BEYOND THE EYES

A Collection of Poems

Dr Babu Ram

Copyright © 2018
Library of Congress, Copyright Office,101 Independence Avenue
SE, Washington, D.C. 20559
ISBN 9781729083383

Contents

Preface 11
Acknowledgements 12
About the Author 13
Introduction 14
    A Prayer 15
    to Goddess of Knowledge, ... 15
    Wisdom, Art, and Culture 15
    A Prayer for Difficult Times 18
Nature 18
    The Veil of Nature 18
    Angel Oak 19
    Purple Flowers 20
    The Breeze and Buds Speak 21
    My Blue Sky Days 22
    Butterflies Dream 24
    The Spectacle of Seagulls 25
    Teenage Curiosities 25
    The Flowers Know it all!! 26
    Muir Redwoods 27
    A Snapshot of Life in an Alien World 28
    The Blind Man, ... 30
    Woods, Passion, Happiness, and Solitude 30

- Maple's Mantra 31
- Journeys 32
  - A Journey of Dreams 32
  - The Vacation Time 33
  - The Journey of Moon 34
  - The Diary of Voyager I 36
  - A Journey to Yosemite Valley 38
- Seasons 41
  - Monsoon Rains 41
  - Spring's Splendor 42
- Love and Family 43
  - The Eyes Meet and Speak 43
  - The Love 44
  - The Love of My Love 46
  - Lover's Place 47
  - Red Bishop 48
  - A Cuckoo's Coo 50
  - Marriages of Convenience 51
  - Nuptial Ties 52
  - You are my Moon! 53
- Hope 54
  - Hope in Combat 54
  - An Eternity of Hope 55
  - Flame 57
- Friendship 58
  - But Coffee First 58

- Is this Friendship Real? 59
- Celebrations of the Loved Ones 62
  - Mother's Day -I 62
  - Mother's Day-II 64
  - Father's Day 65
  - Flying Colors 66
- Fame 68
  - If you know yourself, the world will know you 68
  - The Road to Eternal Fame -I 68
  - The Road to Eternal Fame-II 70
- Women 71
  - I am a Farm Girl 71
  - The Evening Train 73
  - Pregnancy, Uterine 75
  - Environment, and Embryonic Rights 75
  - Cruelty 77
  - Celebrating Women's Day! 79
- War 80
  - My Oriental Lily: Peace 80
  - A Violinist in a War Zone 81
  - The Big Five 83
- Misdemeanor 84
  - Everybody has a Silly Point! 84
  - Procrastination 87
  - Gossips 88
  - Rumors-I (Females) 89

- Rumors-II (Stampede) 90
- Rumors III (Society) 90
- Rumors IV (Business) 91

Negative Emotions 91
- Temptations 91
- Anger 92
- The Obese Mind 93
- Ethos 95

Society 96
- These People Need to Pause! 96
- Identities clash 97
- The Vote Bank 100
- Campaign Money 100
- Elites 101
- Bullies 102
- Law 102
- Elite Culture 103
- The Post-Truth Life 104
- The Temple Trust is in Breach of Trust 104
- Self-Styled God Men 106
- The Old Man and the Queue 107
- Corruption 108
- Bad Cops, Good Cops 109

Global Threats 111
- Inequalities 111
- Poverty 112

- Immigrants 113
- Refugees 114
- Nuclear War 114
- Water War 115
- Religious Intolerance 115

Terror 117

Terror is a threat to global peace and security 117

- Breeding Fields of Terror 117
- The Phalanx of Negative Minds 118
- Silence Screeches in Pain 119
- Cruelty of Time versus Terror 120
- Hate 122
- Liabilities of Hate 122

Fear 123

- The Demon of Fear – Part I 123
- The Demon of Fear - Part II 124
- Who Fears None? 125

Men, Rivers, and Seas 125

- By the River Narmada 125
- The Ganges is sick and unhappy 127
- The Nile is Sad 128
- The Sea, Waves, ... 129
- Clouds of Liberty, and Sailors 129
- Vanity 129

Water 131

- Water is life and Life is Water 131
- The Tradition of Sharing Water 132
- Men and Wildlife 133
  - Shadows 133
  - Poaching Under Clouds 134
- Liberty and Leadership 137
  - Breeze of Liberty 137
  - Leaders Do Dumb Things! 139
  - Voters Do Dumb Things too! 143
  - They Fear Will Lose the Election 144
  - Should We Trust Such a Leader? 144
  - A Giant of History 146
  - Between Giants and Dwarf 147
  - Shooting in a Texas Church 148
- Motivation 149
  - Desires and Dreams 149
  - Willpower 150
  - Knowledge 151
  - Action versus Inaction 151
- Empathy 153
  - The world will be a better place 153
  - to live for everybody 153
  - Discriminatory Empathy 154
  - Case of Marathwada Farmers 155
  - Case of Street Dogs 156
  - Doesn't Nature Deserve an Empathy? 158

- Darkness 159
- Else Change your Template 160
- Living without Grace 162

Beyond the Eyes 163
- Time 163
- Breath 164
- Eternal Rest 165
- Eternal Matter 165
- Eternal Beats 166
- Eternal Fragrance 166

Preface

Human lives are essentially transitory in nature. We are here on this planet for a limited time. We love certain things and certain people or dislike them. We react to situations based on our superficial and shallow sight rather than discerning and probing the situation at hand.

The human eyes have limitations to see beyond a certain range. The dark matter makes up a vast array of the universe, but it is not visible to the human eyes. Likewise time exists in space, but it is intangible to the human eyes. Facial expressions can be read, but thoughts are completely invisible to the human eyes.

Where the eyes stop to comprehend, poetic imaginations take the journey of human experience forward. Through one's thoughts, a poet has the ability to see things beyond the eyes, unravel the human emotions, perceive the beauty, and experience the joy, and ecstasy of love. A poet discovers the hope in eternity for the benefit of human kind. The same poet also explores toxic emotions that give way to darkness and goad human beings into isolation, greed, injustice, violence, terror, and loss of life.

As far as the thoughts enable one to see through, one is able to see things far beyond the eyes, and thus, expand the realm of human consciousness. In the words of Shri Rabindranath Tagore, India's first Nobel Laureate in literature," an individual's reality is measured by the scope of his or her consciousness. The tracts of spaces he owns don't measure the reality." Reality is influenced by notions based on cultural and religious affiliations, birth conditions, beliefs and faiths, and the environment. The universal reality, which is a manifestation of pure consciousness, is only comprehensible through pure love.

In an attempt to expand the scope of my consciousness, I write poems on a wide range of themes in cultural and socio-political milieu with universal appeal, drawn on the experiences and observations at different locations of the world including but not limited to India, USA, the U.K., China, and the nations of Africa where I lived and worked.

I shared these poems with readers worldwide through my Facebook page on Poetry and Blog. This book came to life based on numerous requests from friends and individuals who asked me to compile these poems so that they could find all of them in one place, and read at their own leisure. Beyond the Eyes is a collection of these and others poems that I have written over a period of 5 years. This compendium should assist in the extension of human consciousness and bring hope and happiness to readers.

Acknowledgements

The author is grateful to Mr. Gerd Altmann for permission to use the image shown as the cover page of the book (ref. email date June 11, 2018). I thank Sneh my wife for inspiration. Sandra's suggestions to group poems by themes are thankfully acknowledged.

About the Author

Dr. Babu Ram is a professional engineer. He worked as Chief Power Engineer at the African Development Bank. In 2016, he left the Bank to pursue his academic and literary interests. He is an Indian citizen and a United States permanent resident.

Introduction

A Prayer to Goddess of Knowledge, Wisdom, Art, and Culture

O! Mother Goddess
I plead you with ten fingers joined,
You may kindly dwell in my mind.
My mind is restive
Like a monkey
It jumps from the ground zero to an attic.
And from one attic to another, and then lands on to a tree.
It is a creature, which is fearless and free.
O! Mother Goddess.
With ten fingers joined
I invite you again to dwell in my mind,
I am confident,
You can make my mind tranquil.
That will help me to scale the gentle hill.

O! Mother Goddess, please dwell in my mind,
I pray you with ten fingers joined.
As
I am unable to sublimate my anger into kindness;
I don't know to change the greed into compassion;
And I do not know how
To turn the lust into an yearning for solace under your feet;
Therefore, with ten fingers joined, O! Mother Goddess.
A refuge in your bosom I truly seek.
You are the embodiment of knowledge, and wisdom; and
You benedict your children in nuances of art and culture.
Which you alone could bestow upon me,
And like others,
You won't ridicule my demand.
And you wouldn't ask me to enroll in the college.
O! Mother Goddess,
With ten fingers joined
I invite you to dwell in my consciousness which is drowned
In the mud of unknown wetlands,

It is unclear, like an uncut diamond
Which is precious, but in it the impurities abound.
It excels in the differencing arts.
This is mine, and that is yours!
It is confused between secular and religious thoughts.
The day and night, it generates impulses, with dangers fraught.
Draped in the lust,
It usually gets the deposits of indelible rust.
I often get angry, and greedy.
Therefore, I seek your grace, and a remedy.
The temptations cloud my consciousness.
And that is why in my heart, I implore your benign presence.
O! Mother Goddess.
I need you more than others.
Because they are sailing near the coast,
And I am at my wit's end, and lost,
In the deep sea, I am left alone.
I stand on the deck of ship, which is sinking.
And in this dreadful night
I am gazing stars, which are twinkling,
I cry for help,
If you don't rescue me,
In the atmosphere like a meteor,
I will burn.

A Prayer for Difficult Times

The debris in the environment reddens the eyes of a man.
He cries for help
As his vision blurs.
None but She hears his voice.
The man gets help out of the blue.
It is said that in the difficult times,
The unexpected source extends a helping hand,
For which we have no clue
If our intent and aim are pure.
That is, while pursuing dreams,
We bear no grudge; no prejudice; no malice; and no envious sore to anyone.

Nature

The Veil of Nature

Nature was lying hidden, but it desired that it be known.
With a mere thought, there was light all over blown.
And thus, began a noble deed of the creation.
It was the first phenomenon of primordial nature and eternal sensation.
The nature revealed her beauty in males, females, flowers, fruits, panoramic views of mountains and seas;
In vibrant colors, melodic songs that colorful birds sing, and in peace and serenity, to name a few.

Imagine, if the nature had veiled her beauty,
There would have been no god of love;
There would have been no sins and virtues;
There would have been no thoughts, words, designs, and colors; and
There would have been no desire, joy, love, romance, life and festivity.
The human imaginations would have suffered a permanent disability.

We would have lived in the perpetual darkness.
And to get over the boredom,
We would have implored the nature to unfold for our benefit the phenomenon of eternal reality;
And to reveal to us her true self, character, and kindness.

However, the nagging noise does not let us connect with the eternal reality.
It does not let us hear the beats of the universe.
We want to do everything and anything in our life time,
But spare a few moments in silence, and solitude to connect with eternity.

Angel Oak

In pride and joy, I stand tall on my strong limbs and bones.
In my blood circulates the killing spirit against powerful storms.
The thing that makes me live a lot longer than man is still arcane.
My deep-entrenched roots give me the trust and confidence.
The male and female energies are active inside my body, but sit in silence.
I procreate alone and my titans grow like me in total brilliance.

The children sit near my trunk and close their eyes, in meditation, to hear the sounds.
They wonder if I could see them, birds in the nest, and squirrels that sprint around.
Lizards and fungi vying to look great in the children's eyes tell them to play safe and sound.
Under my shade, they feel inspired and murmur the wish-fulfilling prayers.
They want an extra-ordinary life, one that is exceptional and rare.
Like me, in their old age, they want to look glorious, accomplished, and inhale fresh air.

Owls complain me over the loss of their habitats, safe haven and food supply.
As snakes need them too, rodents should be given freedom to alter genomes to multiply.
In their weekly sermons, Owls talk about disequilibrium in the eco-system in order to imply.
I asked a young man, did you hear sounds under the Oak?
He said that noisy rains were overwhelmingly making him block;
And wailing children amid the nasty rains gave him a stroke.

Purple Flowers

As I close my eyes, I see a discus
Emit colorful rays,
The spirit of the dawn boosts the beauty of the bay.
The rays melt deposits
Upon entering in of the soul,
Like fire consuming a lump of charcoal.

In my fantasy, I feel presence of lady of the dawn.
Totally dumbfounded, makes me her graceful look.
Which dissolves worries like salt dissolves in the water.
The fuzziness and confusion are over.

The spring sun glitters the land, and hills,
As well as the moods, after a harsh winter.
Dry buds collect some chlorophyll.
Little by little the buds turn purple.
A peacock lectures the buds about beauty, and grace.
Does it make sense to live without the grace? It wonders!
 One fine morning, the buds burst into laughter:
The honeybees hum around to pick nectar.
Barefooted, little Aadi, gallops on the grass; tells me about his mission to Jupiter.

The morning rains make the flowers poised, clean, and smarter.
They smell pleasant like a lady after her shower.
The droplets making a necklace of pearls on the leafs that entice a squirrel
Which wearing it, climbs up on a tree, and hops from one branch to another.
Seeing the spectacle, little Rayva laughed.

The green grass to fix the brown patches orders a concealer.
Pushed by wind, the purple flowers dance in splendor.
The emotions spurt, when a person, is hurt for none of her fault.
Babies do, but don't cry the planets.
The purple flowers heal the broken hearts.
Dispensing the love and hope to people who want those most.

The Breeze and Buds Speak

The morning breeze sings:
Some bloom early; some bloom late.

Everybody will have its time; everyone has a fate.
Buds, look!
You cannot be flowers if you don't know how to bloom.

You have to begin a journey
Even though it is late.
Adversaries and hate obstruct the journey.
While the adversaries try to entrap,
The hate disfigures the face of hope.
However, the hope survives
Like a lamp
The onslaught of thunderous storms.
The power of will makes us strive and win over the adverse circumstances.

But the hopelessness smolders:
And have the buds think aloud.
Even if the buds bloom, the flowers will eventually disintegrate;
 Or
The fear of unknown makes the buds frustrate.
A florist will cut flowers to sell in the market.
The rains come; buds look poised, fresh, and clean.
They reject the fear that plays a villain.
The buds say to breeze, we will definitely bloom
Come what may;
Come again tomorrow,
Our fragrance will like to ride on your back;
And travel far off places to let people know
About the buds have bloomed in the valley.

My Blue Sky Days

A teenager is worried about smog, and this is what he says:

I want back my blue sky days,
Plenty of sunshine and no smog.

I want fresh air and my heydays-
Therefore, restore my city's sagging image.

You know about the real issue, the smog cancels my imaginative flights.
The turtles turn pale, for dwindling of the entertaining sights.
The worrisome waves are hesitant about arriving at the shore.
The migratory birds are unwilling to knock at our door.

I want the humans to unmask their nostrils and breathe in freedom.
Their physical health is to be free from the pangs of respiration.
There is merit in providing them the invaluable hope than despair.
It is better to say this straight, and clear the mist in the air.

The smog forces people to bear incalculable financial loses.
And inconvenience to undertake an emprise and chores
The smog is an alert message:
It indicates that a hacker engages in disrupting Mother Nature's equilibrium.

I wish to save the city and planet from this possible pandemonium.
Is it possible to filter the air from the smog and haze?
They may distribute masks and filters in order to prevent the public rage.
These measures are unlikely to eradicate such a huge problem.

There is need to think a permanent fix to change the situation.
There is also need to invoke the rules of ethics:
Which supports life's foundation and fabrics.
Don't throw your rubbish into your neighbor's yard;
Don't eject the untreated smoke in the atmosphere.
Don't pump the untreated water into the sea and rivers.
Because its consequences, all will bear!

Butterflies Dream

The butterflies dream little things and fly.
In dreams, they are flamboyant and not shy.
They takeoff small flights in their little universe.
They fly, hop and fly again; and again, and relax.

Their dreams rest on tiny pillars of their imaginations.
In between flights, they offer themselves a rest and relaxation.
They decrypt what a flower tells them and to a honey bee.
They enjoy being chased by children and their glee.

They catch airwaves, interact and inform about headwinds.
Before flying, they let the storm cool-off and rescind.
They hate the freezing winter but shine in the colorful spring.
They listen to the nature's radio, play, dance and sing.

The butterflies inspire teenage curiosities
As to what shapes the fashion and the high street realities;
And what lies beyond the insatiable lust for money, sex and pleasure;
And why in the world is there so much fear, violence and anger?

The butterflies speak to the clouds through the rising vapors.
Rains come to liberate minds from the rigidities, and cool down anger;
And advise people to not judge others by their name, color and appearance;
And help learn about genuine opulence.

The butterflies tell us to dream before you fly.
It should be your passionate dream and not a lie.
Don't be fixated on working without sleep for material gains.
Relax a little bit when you should and when you can.

The Spectacle of Seagulls

What do they search when they gaze into the eyes of viewers?
Do they know?
Does anybody know?
I know what I look for in the eyes of others.
I search for twinkling stars in their eyes.
Those shine their lives.
And they could shine mine as well!

The stars smile.
I return the smile to them.
It is of no use to economize on smiles.
Rather it is smart to expend and use our smiles.

The stars transmit streams of light.
It is not blue but ultra-white.
It illuminates the dark alleyways of my heart.
It shapes the future and films the past.

Let not the sun setting scare you at the bay.
The waves are excited and lit by the rays.
The spectacle of seagulls throbs my heart.
The night is just an interlude before a new dawn.

I tell you a fable of love and passion.
They hold me tight in their arms.
The grip is strong and the touch is warm.
They both inspire and cause no harm.

Teenage Curiosities

A lad in his teens asked me this,
What does the red sun mean?
The sun is the source of our life's existence.
I told him, for instance.

And the color red; what does it mean?
The red color signifies the sun's exuberance.
The redness at the sunrise and the sunset is his credence.
The sun plays hide and seek in the winter
When it peeps through clouds, we love the appearance.

How could I see the air was his next question?
I said, you can feel it while breathing in and out, if you pay to it attention.
The other way to view the air is to see the trees being blown away by the air.
It can also run a pump to water the fields of corn.

He said, "Oh I know!" it is a kind of a paper windmill.
Whose colorful blades rotate and spin a feeling of thrill.
In the freezing temperatures, the wind drills down our nostril.
The creeks freeze, while frogs sleep in the tunnel.

This teenage friend joins me walk through the wild vegetation,
We enjoy herbs and flowers and their aromatic sensation.
The herbs have medicinal values is an interesting territory.
His teenage curiosities inspire me to tell his story.

The Flowers Know it all!!

The flowers know that they are to live for few days!
They are not worried from appearance, everyone says.
They bloom; dream; and radiate colors and fragrance.
No craze, no crave, and they lead life in absolute brilliance.

Wow! An anxious soul, pauses for a moment, looks at, and exclaims.

The flowers never wander in search of name.
Though we give them a name- rose or jasmine.
Golden sunny rays kiss and make the dawn splendid.
At dusk they rest in the pristine valley of kings.

The grass sings praise, rising on the wings of winds reach everywhere.
Rough weather is harsh for the flowers too.
Yet, the flowers shine as usual, all time.
The flowers speak subtle, brief and benign.

To get what they say, we have to open the eyes of our mind.
The dove perched nearby picks what a flower says:
Try to be, it is not impossible, a rose or jasmine,
Without harming or pushing aside anyone.
If not, just be like tiny little yellow flowers bedecking a meadow.
They too look pretty; but it is just that their value only few people know.

Muir Redwoods

Everybody enjoys walking through redwoods; everybody loves laughing;
Everybody gets some inspiration; everybody inhales the pure oxygen;
Everybody wants to have fun; and these are some of the things they have in common.

Very tall trees proudly display their stature; they say they are invaluable assets of nature.
Redwood trees tell us to grow tall; to choose a sustainable life style; and

Provide some shade and oxygen to those on whom the destiny is not so kind.

The caves prompt visitors' excitement and awe.
Over two thousand five hundred years ago a young prince, –
Gautama, set in such a cave,
And received enlightenment.
As if caves invites us to come in, sit, and get awakened.

The Cathedral Grove is where one enjoys the nature's serenity and radiance.
The creek tells us to keep going without being worrisome.
The grand owl quietly records the redwood's history.

Redwoods cook their meals in the open hearth of sun.
They don't bake potato, sausage and bun.
They just make their food without fuel being burnt.

The wildfires in their neighborhood scare the Muir Redwood residents.
They want an insurance against the likelihood of such incidents.
Because the wildfires are frequent in the vicinity and remain unabated.

Elsewhere, men burn woods to clear land to increase the area of cultivation;
Such practices create drought, erode soil and cause denudation.
Burning forests is not desirable for whatever is the reason.

A Snapshot of Life in an Alien World

Life was short of the unfulfilled desires.
The culture was bearing a Jacaranda attire.
There was no promiscuity and porosity of love.
The sky was filled with colorful pigeons and doves.

The display of pigeon's game was a delightful sport.
The women were warriors of a different sort.
There was no darkness in the human heart.
Every day was a day of festivity of love and light.

Days had cheesy attractions and nights bore a purple gown.
The spring sprinkled colors over the hills,
Sand dunes hosted jackals; and served them each with a bowl of termites.
A rivulet offered muddy and fibrous drinks to the wildlife, while an eagle had a snake's bite.

Love was planted in the greenhouse of mutual respect and complete devotion.
It was matured by the warmth of sizzling trust, in the cozy conditions.
It manifested in extreme madness in the idol of passion.
Though it happened by choice, there was a serendipitous connection.

The villages were republics and there were no voiceless in the town.
Justice was quick and delivered free; and the freedom flourished on the lush green grounds.
Symbols were kept out, and the ideas of substance rewarded.
People were selfless, means were not unfair, and empathy for others as value was recognized.

There was no King Priest, no mother queen, no courtesans and dancing girls.
The life was simple, adorable, and free from enigmatic puzzles.
The women were treated as angels of love, hope, desire with dignity.
Everybody got an equal share from a barrage of opportunities.

The songs of natural beauty were written, sung and praised.

The bubbles of emotions, in the Jacuzzi of reasons, were born and lost.
The warmth of hearts kept alive the yearnings of universal happiness and hope.
Lit by the sun, misty heights and flowery meadows gave impressions of a color Kaleidoscope

The Blind Man,

Woods, Passion, Happiness, and Solitude

A blind man lives alone in the woods.
Come spring, a creek flows in his neighborhood.
His companions are his dog, a cat and a violin.
His cottage stands on the wooden pylons.

His neighbors are all kinds of creatures.
He lives in absolute harmony with nature.
He plays violin every now and then.
Every day, be it a dry or rainy.

The melodious violin mesmerizes animals.
They express joy in simple and subtle ways -.
The elephants dance; lions cuddle lambs.
Animals drink the creek water and thank.

The ants trek to collect grains of millets.
They return mouthful stored in their billets.
The squirrels toil like ants to ensure food in the rain.
The reckless crows unheeded the advice of the blind man.

He plants trees on the trails out of courtesy to pedestrians.

He cleans creeks every spring out of passion.
The blind man's love is to work for public good.
But to him, the nature is at times, unkind, rough and rude

Food to birds is his basket's load.
To get milk supplies he rears a goat.
The greedy crows hover over his basket;
They try to snatch the sweet balls from his pocket.

Smelling the food, monkeys go crazy.
The morning is a bit wintry and hazy.
The blind man with arms sleeves up and smiles,
 Embraces them all in their style.

The blind man enjoys his solitude.
What matters to him is not money but attitude
Toward life, community, fields and natural creeks.
His life is amazingly happy, inventive. He is humble and meek.

The silence opens his heart's treasury.
Unruly elephants and roaring lions never make him jittery.
He never needs a gun to guard from the fellow beings.
His weapon is unconditional love and humility instead of guns.

Maple's Mantra

Whereas people celebrate the spring,
 I celebrate my life during the fall.
I stand straight and tall.
I don't scramble like others to buy fame.
Nor do I beg anyone to remember my name.
Everybody likes my golden color.
They enjoy my gown's glamour.

My aura inspires folks.

And relieves them from the stressful shock.
As they dissolve their ego and frustration,
They ride on a chariot of imaginations.

I will drop my leaves, I know, soon
But the nature tells me to carry on.
The tales of my charm travel beyond the oceans.
I receive friends and enjoy their admiration.

I tell folks to live every day of life full
Though some days are dark and dull.
The spring's splendor is great, and special.
But looking beautiful in the fall is graceful.

Journeys

A Journey of Dreams

Billions of people dream.
But the road to dreams
If there is one, is kind of a dirt road.
Boulders and potholes block the road.
Though the destiny paves it,
The action is great.
Those who don't decide or perform, fall into oblivion.
Successes grace only those with an indomitable spirit; and
Supported by a non-malleable willpower
The action surmounts every obstacle on the way to the dreams.

Everybody dreams of love, wealth, fame and name.
The dream gives life a purpose.
There are blind curves;
You have to take a calculated risk.

There are no gains without a loss.

Pursue your dreams.
However, if you don't succeed,
Before compromising to temptations and compulsive monetary deficits,
Pause a little bit.
Think of the temptations:
Desires, love and lust lay a trap.
The penury conditions reinforces the trap.
Never can a ship reach a shore
That has sailed without a compass.

Being insecure and anxious,
In rush, you will damage the safety valves.
The directionless journey of a dreamer reaches a dead end.
So never give in to fear and temptations and give up your dream.

Don't be fearful of people, neighbors, friends, and even foes.
They will anyway, pass a judgment and innuendo on you.
Do not live with such people around you.
Live for yourself.
Original ideas are recipes for recognition and fame.
Copycats fail despite their big names.

The Vacation Time

It is the summer time
We flew down to our planet's remote corner.
Here, the life revolved around canoeing, fishing and foreigners.
There were plenty of blue water lakes, beautiful beaches and more.
Young and old couples landed in hordes;

They seemed to like the happy faces on the shore.

High waves, warm sand, and cool breeze welcomed the vacationers.
The blue water on which our canoe sailed suddenly became rough.
Rowing against the current was really troublesome and tough.
Our brave hearts rode on the roaring waves
To the onlookers' sensation, and awe.

The sunshine mystically healed the body from pain.
Everyone had the skin tanned.
Everybody had time to smile, relax, entertain, and be entertained.

The hands held around the waists amid the thunderous pour.
A musical band whipped emotions tuned to a romantic lore.
The belly dance performance attracted everyone's attention.
The courteous service, brochettes, and sparkling wine
Relieved the stiff tissues of neck, shoulders, and spine.

The human beings age; the old age disables them.
A granny had wrinkles all over enjoyed hot snacks and a drink.
Better is joy as the life is short and uncertain, and it may end in a blink.
In the melodrama of life, everybody hankers after love, lust, longing, and lure.
But it is difficult to find a love which is stable, pious, copious, and pure.

The Journey of Moon

I am a blue eyed boy of the earth and sky.
It is a pity; I don't have a dress;

I shiver due to cold,
Don't I deserve a pair of trouser, shirt, hat, and coat?

At my mother's command
I travel all over the places;
And illuminate the plains, huts, hills, seas, and woods.
I reach out the victims of violence, hatred, and grudge.
I shine the faces at a baby's birth.

I am the beauty of the sky,
As I rise in full splendor,
The moods turn romantic and faces glow.
The couples before me make a wish, and bow.

The stars witness my journey.
They tease and ask me, why shouldn't I marry?
And live life as humans do;
And experience the love, romance, and family.

I also appear like a blue moon, and a super moon or blood moon sometimes.
I light up the Himalayan Mountains;
Traveling along the Ganges,
I reach Benares-a city of mysticism.
I give life to aging priests, worshippers, and bathing hubs.

I peep in the gorges of the Blue Nile,
Like a paper boat I sail in the White Nile.
And via Khartoum I reach the Aswan barrage.
In nearby holy land, I shine a mosque and temple wall;
But the air in the holy land is hot, hateful and charged.

I shine the ancient Pyramids; and Sphinx.
I wonder what is it that causes the city of Venice to sink.
I like masks sold in Venice.
Though they hide the facial expressions,

The female mask is about the beauty;
And the male one tells about the felicity.
Between the beauty and happiness, the essential thing is love.
The love is not guaranteed born without a sincere desire, friendship, and mutual trust.

I cross the Atlantic Ocean;
I shine the American valleys, plains, mountains, deserts and shores.
America is made as it stands today, by wisdom, and valor of her people.
Their sacrifices defeated tyranny;
And they cultivated harvests of liberty and democracy.
They gifted them a blessed nation under God.
People enjoy freedom responsibly.
The breeze of liberty blows:
The scientists unfold mysteries of nature on this planet, in the inter-planetary space, and in the universe.
The breeze of liberty inspires them to create the art, music, culture, and literature, vibes of which are heard not only in America but also by the other nations and nationalities who habitat the planet.

The Diary of Voyager I

Two things inspired me to write this piece. (1) The technology of Voyager I to generate energy to continue its journey, and (2) a song in the golden record (KAHAN JAT HO (Where are you going alone? a Mother asks her teenage boy who she thinks, will not return back).

The song is a recording of very famous Kesar Bai Kerkar (1892-1977), an Indian classical vocalist in Raga Bhairavi.

The time to me, seems to have stopped.
My days and nights; somebody has robbed.
My earthly bonds are about to be broken.
I am narrating this truth hitherto unspoken.

I am out on a journey to explore the truth from a distant shore.
I relay what I see; and do not tell any anecdotes and folklore.
I see asteroids and planets from a close range in their splendor.
I am opening a new window to peep deep in the universe, isn't that spectacular?

I have seen the sun hiding under the blanket of the night;
And the moon's rise to glitter the sky is with privileges and rights.
The moonlight throb the hearts of young couples locked in their arms.
The moonlight purifies their emotions, love, and life, and mutual charm.

Seeing the moon's popularity on the earth, the stars grumble in the sky.
The comets sensing the rage begin to cry.
They approach the sun for mediation
The sun told them, "Do not worry"; it is a temporary incident of a short duration.

As I reach near and pass the sun, I felt unusual heat and burns.
I continue my flight, despite several twists and turns.
I have a continuous shower of cosmic rays in the vast universal pool.
However, my thermocouples and isotopes keep me cool.

I am racing to explore the unknown in the intergalactic space.
I see nothing but clouds of cosmic dust, and brownish haze.
I often hear a pulsating sound of a cosmic band.
I look out for a planet of new civilization, in order to land.

A Journey to Yosemite Valley

The voicemail buzzes,
I try to listen,
There is a hissing sound,
But it's not intelligible.

From the deck
I see a river in the valley.
Offering a pleasurable sight.
To weary eyes
Tired of tension and heat.
And eyes happily enjoy the feast.

And above us is the blue sky.
Gifting us a day, bright and sunny.
Colors décor birds, squirrels and bunnies.
Their images still run deep in the memory.

Mountains stand high side-by-side.
Like sleeping giants
Since millions of years,
In the same posture.
They envy the river,
Which doles out water to people, fields, and reservoirs.
The mountains wonder, why cannot they move like the river?

The weather appears to change,
The air turned stuffy and grey.
The tacky smoke
Begins piercing in the lungs and eyes, with coughs and tears.
It seems that woods are burning.
Animals and humans are running away from the spreading fires.
Look at the trees,
It is a pity that they cannot escape the fury of the fire.

The temperatures rise;
So does the haziness in the valley.
Welcoming the vacationers
The road closing signs appear at the junctions.
Vehicles congregate.
The traffic jams are not benign.
Ducking the traffic,
A squirrel crosses the road,
By walking over an overhead cable,
And it chirps,
The traffic is your destiny.

Joining a caravan of hundreds of vehicles becomes our take.
It is not a choice to show the back.
Vehicles are crawling at a snail's pace,
An hour's drive gives two miles.
But there is no chaos,
No rat race;
No road rage;
No overtaking; and
No honking.
Everyone is driving with grace.

Finally, the Yosemite Valley reaches out to us.
The Yosemite waterfall welcomes us.
The people-young and old, tourists and locals;
Infants, toddlers and teenagers

Come, view, and love the waterfall.
They become awestruck by the spell of nature's beauty,
By the peace, the pleasure, and the site's serenity.
Cameras roll.
Everybody captures.
The moments of peace, love, and beauty.
The waterfall shows us a mirror.

It is dusk time.
Slowly darkness prevails in the valley.
The moon appears, rising below the mountain.
People rush to restaurants, and grab whatever they can.
On the table, crispy pizzas shine.
The laughter blends the wine.
The hungry cubs, lionesses and lions,
Celebrate the success of the journey at dinner time.

Whether it is this journey or another,
It does not matter.
Keep striding ahead,
Accept,
There will be crowds.
There will be traffic jams.
There will be heat, humidity and sweat.
And irritations of all sorts.
But don't show your back.
And don't let your grace fall during the journey.
Ultimately,
The mountains move;
And
Patience pays;
Perseverance pays;
Courage pays;
And conviction definitely pays.

Seasons

Monsoon Rains

The clouds look overjoyed in the sky,
Like in a cocktail party,
The ladies and gentlemen rub their shoulders
The gray clouds do the same with the dark ones,
And it pours rain with lightning and thunder.

The thunder robs a fetus of sleep in her mother's womb.
Only does the fetus know the flashpoints of the day inside the womb.
The mother's face turns pale, thinking that
The baby might be frail.
But over the fear, the hope always prevails.

The lightning gallops in her venture to kiss the earth.
Caring least about burns it will cause to humans, and herbs; and
The nests and dreams.
Defying the odds, a Cuckoo rebuilds its habitat without any scream.

The monsoon rains make everyone happier.
The minds shade despair:
The dust-laden leaves look a lot fresher, and greener.
The trees shine just as the faces do,
Over the rounds of 'Hilsa' cubes and a glass of wine.

It drizzles, though people assemble to work out in the public park
The " Hee -Hee", "Ha -Ha" and "Hoo -Hoo", of the "laughter Yoga",
Uplifts the spirit of men, and women.

"If you want to improve your health, you can" is in the air.
The message is well understood, but not spoken.
The farmers are rolling up their sleeves
To prepare fields to sow paddy and corn.
The Monsoon rains make everybody heaves a sigh of relief.
The weatherman so prays to the heavens that the rains should not be brief.

Spring's Splendor

I ask the flowers, what is it that makes them look so beautiful in the eyes of beholders?
They say, they always smile, shirk melancholy, and
spread fragrant flavors.
And they attract views for their eye catching colors.
They are beautiful because they search for beauty within them.
Just as by digging deeper in the earth, a miner finds a few gems.
Unlike a musk dear which, though roves for the same search, finds none.

No wonder, the arrival of spring after harsh winter, is welcomed by everyone.
The breeze of spring knocks at the entirety of nature.
And the nature's bloom is viewed by hordes of lovers.
The god of love launches the love-laden kites,
Decorates sky with colorful sights.
The kites kindle fire in the hearts of buds,
Which swell into flowers.

 As beauty unveils, even on an Ascetic's forehead,
sweats appear.
The spectacle threatens to breach the embankments of desires.

Before glamor and beauty, unconditionally surrender the desires.
As the eyes peep into eyes, the flowery faces smile.
And say, the idea of love is worth pursuing for a while.

Ascending the pinnacle, the love shuns every perfidy.
Like what a moth does around the lamp,
The love swirls to radiance of the beauty.
It forsakes its identity.
That helps the love in extending its realm to infinity.

Love and Family

The Eyes Meet and Speak

Eyes meet and speak love; they drink nectar of love; and they love to drown in the lake of love.
A fountain of love springs forth; water drops fall on couples on the benches of a harbor.
Anxieties disperse just as clouds do upon the thrust of strong winds as they dance in the twilight splendor.
The season of love begins, eyes dream; and hearts spread wings to fly and flutter.

When the eyes meet, it appears the world is frozen, and thinks nobody could see them.
To kiss and love becomes a routine, on the road, in a corner, as there is none in between the eyes to refrain.
The romantic moods like the air touching the red cherries, romanticize an otherwise dull evening.

They swear, their love is forever, but to enjoy it, let there be no perfidy; and let there be no bargain.

Life is a temple which the love lights; a breath's return is to commence a new prayer, and to welcome a new dawn.
Love is idolized in the temple; the temple gets a face lift; and eyes blow a conch heralding a new era of love and romance.
Eyes say "no" to rude stares, and refuse to flirt with waves on the shore in the violent ocean.
But strong winds cast a shadow of fear to prompt the eyes to unite; and the love continues through the night.
The seashells help the eyes to track down the imprints of their love, which are left untouched by the storm.

Eyes speak to eyes, get drunk off the love, in boundless space, and take short-to-long flights.
The eyes settle down to the earth, but stars tell to look up to make the love in starry nights.
So as the stars love and shine; they live for the lover, give her eternal gifts and delight.
Speaking to stars eyes tell them, "The love that they see in her eyes is not ephemeral."

The Love

The love is not the greed;
The love is not selfishness indeed.
The love is not about having an excessive pride.
The love is not miserliness.
The love is not theory.
The love is a practice

The warmth of the love melts hearts like stones,
The love, like the moon, lights up the seas, valleys, ruins, and hills unknown.

The love is indifferent to loss and gain; dishonor and fame; and pleasure and pain.

The love like the word of gospel is eternal.
Love creates necessary conditions for cosmic romance, moreover.
Although the entry in the God's garden is restricted,
But the love is a key to unlatch the door.

The love burns ego which otherwise refuses to go.
The love unties knots of ignorance;
The love kills smog of vengeance;
The love bends the iron fist of arrogance.

And the love treads courageously even in chaotic circumstances.
The love celebrates the compassionate thoughts for everybody's happiness.
The love respects human dignity unconditionally.
To love is mandatory, and to return the love with love is humanity.
To love and to be loved is not a choice,
It is an antidote to deceitful vice.

The physics of wealth confines to the earth,
But the metaphysics of the love travels distances beyond the eyes.
The love heals the wounds of insult and injuries;
And the love wipes out the moisture in the eyes.
The love is peace, and the love is an eternal value.
The love is truth; the love is beauty; and to love is godly.

Love bridges the gap between despair and hope;
Love shortens the span between the have and have not.
The love gives a meaning to life.
The love builds resilience to cope with civil and mental strife.
To love is innately humane;

The wealth of love multiplies if it is wisely spent.

The love does not need the two persons to situate close by.
The love does not require the possession of the earth to touch the sky,
The love is a transaction if it proceeds with an "if."
The love is an unconditional plunge into the deep sea from a cliff.

The love is being; becoming is the love; and the love is the ultimate bliss.
The love heals mental agony, frustration, dissatisfaction, and depression.
The love repairs broken hearts.
The love rekindles hope in the patients of the cancer ward.

The Love of My Love

My life before you came in, was like a virgin island,
Yet to be discovered, inhabited, and named.
Though migratory birds landed and nested every season,
It received no human interest to make a home.

The island's beauty was incomparable,
But that was not sufficient to bring happiness.
The breeze of your love displaced the hopelessness and
It made the island a desirous place to live, to enjoy, to hope, and hanker for happiness.

The love has enriched the island.
Which is the life's beginning and the end.
 I am afraid, if you leave me
I will be poor like a barren field.

That is with a lot of space, which without rains of love, gives no yield.
Your love provides me a reason to life and a shield.

I despise missing you,
To love you and live with you is my life's goal.
The thought of living a life without you pinches my soul.
I dream to forever live with you.
My heart will break, if I lose you.
But the beauty, panoramic views, and serenity, the island has nothing to offer you.
As rightly said, the pure love does not need a transactional hue.

You have to dig deep in the heart to fathom my love.
You will find a spark that shines our "two lives and one soul" kind love.
My love flows in your blood stream.
You can sense its warmth in your arteries and veins.
The bodies shrink; and the glow of the faces fades.
The true love lives forever young and does not age.

However,
The anger makes a day of relative peace topsy-turvy.
Tells a voice, to everyday to forsake impulses of hatred and envy.
Whispers a third voice in my ears there is a way to make two persons hopeful and happy.
The one who is at fault should always have to tender an apology.
And the other, to forgive and forget to make the relationship smooth and cozy.
I hope to love you and be loved by you.
But I don't like to live in a cage.
I want the liberty to run my race.

Lover's Place

It is the lover's place.
The air kisses clouds, the river, the sea, and trees.
The clouds kiss a mountain; and the mountains kiss the climbers.
The river kisses every drop of rain, and the sea welcomes every river.
The tree relieves a tired traveler of fatigue; they embrace one another.

The mammals lock up their bodies to warm one another.
The young and old couples lock horns like a pair of deer on every Valentine's Day.
Just as waves crush on the shore every second every day;
Just as a pair of street dogs lick the skins and relax.
Just as monkeys activate their sexuality at the break of the day.

The birds, bats, and owls discuss the love and place to live.
The lightning and thunder destroy their little nests and habitats;
They muster courage, rebuild tiny abodes, and enjoy life and love.

Red Bishop

This poem is inspired by a real incident in our residence in South Africa: A Red Bishop bird weaves a nest at the far end of a branch of a blackberry tree hanging over the swimming pool.

Red Bishop weaves a nest at the far end of a branch over the pool.
The female comes in, dismantles it and flies away, mocking at his tools.
Red Bishop tries again, pulls straw, leaves and grass.
He hurriedly decorates the nests with earthworm droppings.
That this time she would like it, was a Red Bishop's guess.

She felt that making a nest on a stem made it vulnerable to snakes.
And that a serpent would bite her eggs.
Chicks would die before they were born.
She flew, and looked at Bishop in scorn.

This time Red Bishop chose a tall tree and a long and flexible branch.
Not over the pool but over a rose garden.
The blowing winds swing the nest, and push rosy fragrance in.
The nest is the culmination of Bishop's vanity, and female's pride.
That she would dislike is unlikely this time.
Being a perfect abode, the nest is an envy to crows.

She and Bishop come along, play, and exchange vows to remain united.
Love and beauty cook various dishes of desires in the phosphoric light.
At last, she lays eggs.
Being anxious she hovers over and around the nest.

Soon the chicks come out,
With pink cheeks and eyes shut.
While chick's sleeps in the nest,
She flies in search of food toward the woods in the west.
She crosses meadows and creeks.
And she returns with some grains in her beak.

She and Bishop toil to nurture them strong.
Raising them become their mission along.
One day chicks spread the wings;
Soon they are in the world of dreams and in the lap of wind.

When they are exhausted, they fly back to the earth.
But strong winds destroy their home and hearth.

This is a bright sunny day that they descend at my terrace.
They jump on the floor relieving from fatigue and stress.

Beside the pool, they find some kernels that squirrels left behind fearing the rains.
Being hungry and tired, they like the food, as well as the shady cool.
They are happy like shepherds who are happy after they sell their herd's wool.
After eating most and spilling some, they fly away, up in the sky.
At our terrace, we still await them to return and stop by!

A Cuckoo's Coo

It is still dark,
The street dogs still bark.
A Muezzin (a Moslem priest) is calling faithful persons to join him for the prayer.
In a temple, bells are ringing;
And a priest while chanting mantras is performing rituals to the prayer.

Amid this hullabaloo, a little cuckoo,
Perching in a neighborhood garden
Rises just before the dawn.
And sings a melodious Coo, Coo, Coo,
Like an alarm clock,
It alerts anybody who is interested in listening to the beats of the universe
It is the time to wake up, sit and meditate;

Hear the sounds; and inhale a life sustaining positive energy
That every day before the sun rise,
The goddess of dawn radiates.

Hearing the coo
The flowers rub their eyes, smile, and bloom.
The buds will follow them soon.
The hearts of the emotionally charged persons sink.
Only could ladies whose beloved partners are away from them
Understand the link.
The distances dissuade emotions to aspire for unity.
In life's drama, there are happy hours, and there is a scene of tragedy.

While awaiting a call back from the male partner,
The cuckoo is musing:
The moments of joy are few and rare,
The life is filled with many surprises,
The gloomy days arrive without a warning.
Every moment is special and precious to live a passion and desire.
The days of youth are few in numbers.
The old age comes with a stick in the hand.
Everybody needs a hubby to walk by the river, holding hand in hand.

She coos yet again,
This time, the coo is even louder and the successive coos are quick.
Being a heartless partner, he does not return her call.
He just whispers something in the air,
Which the cuckoo is not able to hear.

Marriages of Convenience

Marriages of convenience are built on the foundation of sand and selfishness.
Fear and fraud roost in life; in frictional heat, the love, like camphor, evaporates.

The values say to look for a deceptive signal, but in the cross fire, a signal is dissipated.
Somehow stars decode a signal, the "marriages of convenience" are things they reject.

The politicians hatch the marriages of convenience to eliminate a common foe.
To them, friends and foes are temporary; they change them as the situation show.

They interpret values to suit them; and then display power and sensuous infidelity.
There are luminaries who inspire others by example through selfless service to humanity.

The nations also indulge in the "marriages of convenience" and benefit from their amity.
An influential friend ignores a friend for abusing human right values, but criticizes her adversary.

Rivals squabble; reposition them; and engage in violent attacks with a wolverine's ferocity.
But visionary leaders even out differences and establish on borders, the peace and tranquility.

Nuptial Ties

A bride and a groom, knot their lives, in the presence of sacred fire or at the altar.

They become husband and wife, to lead life, happily until they die, thereafter.

This is a knot of grace; it unites two human beings, and possibly, their hearts.
The knot, in their union, lays the foundation of a family to signify a start.

But the busy life, careers, and no-time for taking care of the other add paraffin to fire.
The depression consumes an appetite for love, and sour, turn the taste of their life.

Patchwork, to sort out knotty revelations, is kind of a temporary fix, and the trust gap, between them, widens.
No surprise, marriages break; numbers of broken marriages or single parent families continue to rise.

You are my Moon!

A toddler boy tells me, "You are my moon"
His words make me smile.
I lift him in the air;
And I give him a hug.

Does he mean it?
Yes,
He does not know the non-truth.
So what he speaks is a plain truth.
His tongue utters God sent words.
The truth reflects beauty inside a mind.

The truth and beauty makes a child divine.

Hope

Embrace the hope, when your heart is experiencing restlessness.
Haven't you seen that the hope has broken the blocks of mind?
Don't you see that the imagination, powered by the hope is flying in the Welkin?
Shouldn't you know just by listening to your heart, nature reveals a pool of possibilities to you?
If your eyes don't see whole, there is problem.
The journey will not succeed without the traction of hope and character that drive life's train.

Hope in Combat

With paltry means, and without jobs, the young men are at war with life in the war zone.
The mine fields and bombs compel them to run away in search of new homes.
The young minds worry about their future. Their anxieties are disturbing and true.
When market forces find their education irrelevant, being worrisome they rue.

Worries are like messy noodles cooked in hot sauce, and if we swallow them hot, the tongue's tender tissues will be burnt. Shouldn't we better handle these noodles little by little with the Chinese patience?

Like thunder comes with rains, the fear, disenchantment and diminution of courage come with worries.
Shouldn't boys sing songs of hope and dance to beats, and work to secure future, rather than indulge in war crimes?

With the fall of night, hope riding a chariot enters the eyes, and a dream is born.
Their willpower gains tempo and a lucky day, they will win against all odds and remove thorns.

An Eternity of Hope

Hope

Hope lives in the hearts of the rich and poor.
The poor aspire for riches and the rich make more.
Hope motivates us in everyday life, to strive and score.
Without hope, the life becomes lifeless, lousy and sour.
The hope nourishes the passion of a vineyard in sundry lives.
It lights a lamp in the hearts broken by a civil war and civil strife.
 Hopelessness robs a man of passion and a woman of her dreams.
The wheels jam as life's locomotive runs short of stream.
The world exists on the pills of hope and humanity.
Hope prepares a fertile ground for peace and tranquility.
Hope drives the dreaming doves to check the hawkish hype in every opportunity.
Hope is a rising sun, and a pole star always shine in absolute punctuality and perpetuity.

Hopes are waves when they enter in my space, I smile like a young flower.
The waves are everywhere: I sense them as I see boldness in the dreams of a doer.
I heard waves in the beats of the African music and in the Nile River and Zambezi's magnanimity.
I found waves in my obscure days; and I still enjoy them, others do as well, in a sense of eternity.
The waves need a shore to rush and reach and a receptor of an open mind and a big heart.
To get your hope you have to give it to others who, in difficult situations, badly need and want.
That hope you can get from yourself, in your life, when you reorient your mind to a right direction.
A single line or an idea from a proverbial wisdom and literature could be a source of an inspiration.

What happens when hopes are shattered?

Tsunami waves, cannot be said to bring hope, as they wreak disasters in towns, fields and basins.
Hopes are shattered, when something sad and bad, which is quite unexpected, before us, happens.
But what follows the destruction, is always reconstruction and resurrection of sagging morale and hope.
The hope rebuilds the edifice of the life systems, and this is how the human ingenuity rises and copes.

Channels of Hope

Hope is not a desire; it is a tool; it is rusted, it needs a sharpened edge to chisel a statue of eternity.
No wonder, the man built them to receive; and received inspiration, hope of freedom, and liberty.
Still, there are injustices; restricted dreams, and inequitable distribution of prospects and opportunities.

Billions of people around the world need hope, and assurance to dream and challenge that impropriety.
What is not transient, and which transcends extremities, should be channels of hope and assurance.

Hopes of the present century are: responsible and ethical leaders, opportunities, clean air, no tear, no fear, and no intolerances.
Young women cannot go to college in their town so they seek education in a different city, due to fear and lack of safety.
Intolerance is still widespread, it is evident from the targeted killings, disappearance of critical voices, terror, ethnic cleansing, and cruelty.
The leaders should give hope by allaying fears, providing safety, and letting constituents dream.
The leaders having failed people's expectations, never come back; get punished at the voting machine.
Parents should give hope to children and an armory to fight injustice, fear and insensible intolerances.
Children should never abandon their parents "at the mountain" when they need most their assistance.

Flame

The flame that burns in the heart creates science, knowledge and art.
It shows a direction to a troubled man
Like a light house indicates direction to a ship.
To muddle through rough waters
And reach the shore.
The flame lets us inhale the positive energy of the universe.
While exhaling, it dumps the dirt out in the universe.
The traveler enjoys every moment of journey.
Because it knows that in the next moment, he or she will be lonely.
He or she loves others indiscriminately,

While eclipsing the hate simultaneously.
Like a wave it rises to hold an unknown hand.
The notions of supremacy the mind disbands.

But when the flame is put out by the carbon
Of extreme hate, anger, pride, and fanaticism,
There flares up emotions of rage and revenge
Making people crazy - the executioners of hate, the knife wielding youths,
Whose actions kill many persons; and
Have countless injured.
The crazy drivers who ploughed vehicles on the tourists killed innocent persons en masse.
How could a vehicle turn to a weapon to murder persons en masse?

Friendship

But Coffee First

It is more than a coffee shop.
It is a place where young girls and boys, and senior citizens assemble.
It is an oasis of green smiles in the red hot desert.
Good friends meet over the coffee; and reject stereotypes and notions.
Its amiable ambiance revives love in the deeply drowned eyes to peep through the hearts.
The coffee arouses feelings and emotions for one another.
The clock continues ticking, so does the coffee machine; it is now time to talk.

Discussing anxieties with friends over the coffee, worries are reduced.
Meeting and greeting friends is strongly beseeched in the era of technology.
But to make an all-weather friend like an all-weather road is not easy.
The physics perishes with the time but the chemistry of love survives to live a long last.
You want to know if I am impressed with your overture,
I will tell you, but coffee first.

It is more than a cup of coffee. It is an opportunity to smoothen relations that are rocky.
It is an occasion to inhale the fragrance of jasmine flowers.
The beautiful ladies adore bracelets and necklaces made of the jasmine flowers.
I take this date as a chance to discuss our love's future.
You propose to me and now you plead for my reply,
I will give you my consent or otherwise, but coffee first.

It is more than a cup of coffee to small farmers.
Producing coffee is family business.
The family drinks coffee together served by the lady of house.
The members exchange pleasantries of love, and smiles.
The home labor sustains the family business.
When a man announces, he is going to the fields,
The spouse simply smiles; hold his hands in her hands; and tell,
Yes, you should my dear, but coffee first.

Is this Friendship Real?

You look nice;

you visit us often;
you come to my home, drink and dine.
Behind my back, to your friends
you speak things about me that are not benign.
Not only this, you also send rumors.
I live through horror.
Is this friendship real?

Today is our anniversary.
You are invited to the party to celebrate us.
Though you meet us every day, but today you do not show up.
You did not join us last year.
The year before last, you pretended to attend to business.
It seems you don't want to be happy in our happiness.
Is this friendship real?

You always criticize me.
You find faults in everything that I do.
When I am well dressed up, you don't look in my eyes.
Instead you look at my shoes.
Is this friendship real?

In the meetings, you are rude,
you cut me short, as I speak.
While others like me.
You leak secrets.
While I am humble, you are a crook.
Your shenanigans,
I can no longer overlook.
Is this friendship real?

While you talk,
you say things only about your home, your blog, and your poems,
your dreams, your hopes, and ambitions.
You don't pause as you paint a picture.
You think we are here to hear you,

you don't realize there are issues in our life
and in our eyes too, occasionally there are tears.
Is this friendship real?

Time is an invaluable asset of life.
You prime your time, while you undervalue my asset.
The time waits none, but you make me endlessly wait.
You make lame excuses and hold on flimsy grounds
As usual you pass the buck to a third person.
Your famous solution that you prescribe for every problem, I still remember,
you will get what you want if it is in your luck.
Is this friendship real?

Even though you have a plenty of money,
you still borrow it from me to not let your savings deplete.
You assume that my home is yours,
But when I press your door bell,
Looking through the magic eye,
You know it is me,
But you don't unlatch your door,
Is this friendship real?

You think you are a man of importance,
and I am your subordinate clause in the party.
Which you invite
me, so you reach out
and talk
but you never walk your talk.
When you see someone more influential than me
Away from myself you surreptitiously slip.
Is this friendship real?

I am your friend, and he is your adversary.
You dare say a word against your enemy in private.
You want to teach him a lesson in theory.

Not by yourself but through me, your friend
who you ask to open fire at your adversary.
You make me, your friend, a scapegoat,
if the conspiracy unfolds,
He would spare you but slit my throat.
Is this friendship real?

Celebrations of the Loved Ones

Mother's Day -I

The inspiration for this poem is (1) a mother and (2) the Mother's day.

The umbilical cord was my connection with her;
I received from and sent encrypted signals to her.
I knew no Twitter, Facebook, at all;
I was floating within and bumping on the wall.

Her good mood inspired me float fast,
Bad mood dampened my spirit aghast.
Her mood often swung like a wild cat.
She abhorred drugs as told by the test.

I lost connection when she slept;

When she woke up, did everything to make me please.
In me, she encoded truth, courage and wisdom;
I was a little prince of her kingdom.

At birth I cried,
The nurse cuddled me and said, I know it is hard to be a baby.
She gave me a feed, as after labor,
My mother was tired, and drained.

Now I am a grown up kid,
I am open but I sometimes play hide and seek.
My mother is unique;
And she is my guide as well a critique.

She patted on my back when I won;
And she encouraged me after the loss.
When I played soccer in the field.
Everybody cheered me, but she provided me an emotional shield.

I am now a college boy,
But the childhood memories are still alive.
Her words of advice are inspirational and wise.
Her blessings hold my hand tight in the dangerous zones;
Her teachings protect from evil forces and fears unknown.

When I return home from college,
She looks at me, and exclaims, wow!
Her love made me what I am now.
She is as gentle as a "Kamdhenu"-a wish-fulfilling cow.

She is my mother.
And she is the best mother in the world!
She is pure honey;
And she sweetens my life's bitter gourd.

I offer her cake, and wine;

But she says that to her my love is fine.
She needs no lies but plain facts.
Her directions are doubtlessly exact.

To family and friends, she is a perfect host.
She is my ultimate refuge when a paradise is lost.
She gives me solace, wine, butter and toast.
And as I bow, she hugs and loves me utmost.

I share her story and genetic touch.
She is rated high by temple, mosque, and church.
Her love for me is genuine.
Under her watchful eyes, I am safe and sanguine.

Mother's Day-II

No mother likes person
When he gives her child pain.
Like a kite, she attacks at an intruder and she refrains.
She ensures her child's safety in the seas, on the hills, and in wild jungles.
She sacrifices so that kids get what they choose.

She desires her children win laurels, and glory.
Her sacrifice is the hallmark of her life's story:
She works for her children's success- takes no break and recess.
She labors silently in the kitchen, and in the fields,
But her contributions are understated in a family's yield.

She calls on God to grant her children valor and wisdom, hope, pleasure and fame.
And God answers her prayers and the children get nearly the same.

The lucky ones join the Army.
To earn bread and butter for the family, and honor for the nation.

They go overseas to fight the extremists and terrorists.
When their journey stunts,
Again she calls on God, raising her hands in prayer.
The children escape unhurt or survive a deadly attack
And thank her for spiritual guidance and care.

Father's Day

The molecular bonds bind a child and father.
It is like spring's fresh air kissing the earth from the atmosphere.
We smile, and grow under his watchful eyes and care.
His Love inspires us to be exceptionally humane and rare.

He hopes that one day, she will bloom like a full moon.
She is blessed by a hermit's boon.
Her smiles relieve him of daily stress and pain.
She feels like a lioness in her father's den.

Love is the sweetness of their genetic mesh.
None can repay him for his care and cash.
His love is unselfish; and cherished are dreams.
He gave us self-esteem that enabled us through many turbulent streams!

He is like the ocean of knowledge, which is unwritten in the books.
He insulates us from the troublesome hooks.
We learn from him many helpful clichés to clinch a century.
Higher than the sky is his glory!

He holds our hand tight in trials and tribulations.
He pats our back when we are in despair and dissolution.

He touches our spinal cord; and rekindles the dampened fire.
His knowledge and wisdom we benefit from and admire.

Unassailable is his character, and he is not greedy.
He teaches us to reach out to serve the needy.
He treks rough terrains, hills and ancient trails.
He builds fortunes with dedication to work and to travail.

He expects us to preserve values and character in our life
In the native land; in an alien world; and in cultures of colorful stripes.
Losing character is like a fallen soldier to never revive.
The losing of an opportunity to strike gold, he dislikes.

He is like copper red sun rising at the dawn;
And he talks about hope and warmth, sitting at his armchair in the lawn.
No doubt, at times, he is hot and angry,
But his love is sweeter than pure honey.

Take time-off to be with your kids on the Father's Day.
Appreciate their every gesture in what they do and say.
Gift your father little things even if they look a bit crazy.
Crack some humor to let him laugh, and take life's challenges easy!

Flying Colors

Desires and Love play "hide and seek."
In the mango groves,
By the side of a creek.
Love gives its victory speech, desires reluctantly accept the defeat.
Angry desires blame the Love, for being rude, unfair and a cheat.
At being insinuated and hurt, the love takes a back seat.

And in silence and solitude,
Love does such things that burn the ego and attitude.
It surrenders to and serves God in servitude.
It expresses to him its gratitude:
It sings a melody;
It serves the poor and needy;
It dances in ecstasy;
And it reads the devotional essays.

The time changes,
And the seasons do the same.
After a sweltering summer, rainy season, winter
Spring comes, and cherry blossom.
Colors fly from the earth to sky.
Nature camouflages codes in the colorful designs.
In shells; in plumage of peacocks; and in the butterflies.

In her unique ways, the nature celebrates the festival of colors.
The folks play, dance, and sprinkle on one another watercolors.
The spectacle entices the love birds,
The flying colors cast a spell;
On their minds like the buzzing of wasps;
Like a magic of fragrances.

The desires resurface,
Like in rainy season frogs wake up.
At the confluence of colors, desires, and beauty,
Love proudly displays its profundity.

Love takes a dip in the aromatic cocktail of colors, desires, and beauty.
That mind majestically hails the dip.
Love wins the play, and desires get the love.
And they together pass a test of fidelity with flying colors.

Fame

If you know yourself, the world will know you

A silent voice whispers in my ears:
Everybody is invaluable, you have to know your worth. If you don't value your worth, none will hold you in esteem.

If you want to do everything, nothing can you completely do.
The show will end; and slapping on your face, the time will bid adieu.
Chose just one thing,
Nobody will tell you, what is that? You must know it and focus on.

If your goal is to know me, and my love, you first have to know yourself.
If you know yourself, the world will know you.

The Road to Eternal Fame -I

The waves perform a liturgical action.
They rise and fall.
The wind helps the waves in the rise.
The waves roar
Like the sea lions
Which enthrall the viewers more and more.
By counting the waves at the shore,

Can anyone measure the depth of the ocean?
No
You have to take a plunge in the sea.
The unshakable faith lifts the human spirit up.
The defeat has no future and face.
The victory is an 'objet d'art' which to the fame, means a lot,
But a person has to play not one but many decisive shots.

The waves inspire everybody
But those who claim a share of fame are celebrities, writers, and scientists.
Like nature when she desires to be known, creates a unique world,
The writers create poetry and fiction before unheard;
The sculptors with their chisels make an image of God which is worshipped;
The cine artists with their crafts entertain the world;
The musicians perform incredible feats:
They light a lamp, and make rains with the power of their music.
The charismatic music engages viewers and listeners spell bound.
The discoveries by scientists unravel mysteries of nature that nurture the world.
If the divinity reveals secrets of the "dark matter" to someone, that will be an epoch making discovery.
These great souls leave behind their signatures and foot prints.
Which stay alive for considerable length of time and breadth in the public memory.
They all have powerful ideas which potentially change the world for good.
The original ideas make these people imminent and famous.
No matter what their craft is,

Everybody has to pass a gauntlet of challenges to stay in the lime light in the public space.

The Road to Eternal Fame-II

There is an opportunity to earn fame in every journey.
The journey, however, has to be performed without an attitude and trickery.
Like "the money follows leaders,"
The fame follows a person of exceptional character and adventures
Who serves to and secures the human kind's future with prejudice to none, in dignity.

The favorable wind helps the sail;
Therefore, in the direction of the wind the sailing is counseled.
However, if the turbulence and headwinds oppose the sail,
You don't have to give up your journey.
Would we have remembered Columbus today, had he abandoned his voyage?

How come a fisherman who ventures in the high seas, returns home empty handed?
How come an unknown fear makes a seasoned batsman nervous only to return to the pavilion with a dismal score?

There is hope for everybody.

The serendipity assists a traveler in mysterious ways;
It tends to compensate a loss:
A person (Stephen Hawking) while sitting on his wheelchair is able to wander in the cosmos.
Serendipity is invisible like a fragrance
Which perfumes the human experience.
The destiny decides the time and quantum of leap.

When the Lady Luck smiles,
She clears blocks on the road to fame.
The public and press recognize the name;
He or she becomes an heir to the throne.
In a royal family, though that person is not born.

Women

I am a Farm Girl

I am strong, sturdy and still.
I live in my farm house in a remote county.
With my parents, siblings, and extended family.
I am a Farm Girl.

I enjoy a long walk and horse ride.
I grow fruits and flowers.
Nature loves me and take care.
I am a Farm Girl.

In my habitat, the music of birds takes no break.
The winds huddle the snowflakes.
Kids throw nickels in the semi-frozen lake.

I am a Farm Girl.

I mind cattle and pigs in the meadow,
Little do they understand me, but follow.
While animals roam freely in the ranch
I read a book sitting on the bench.
I am a Farm Girl.

I think while I am alone.
About my fields of soybean and corn.
I wonder,
What does it make crops grow with little irrigation?
I realize I live in a blessed nation.
I am a Farm Girl.

I do gymnastics and score ten out of ten.
I work in all seasons - sunny, snowing, and rains.
I do a rosary to challenge an evil eye and an intruder's disdain.
I am proud of a farmer's blood that flows in my arteries and veins.
I am a Farm Girl.

In the farm life, the ups and downs are normal.
Gloomy winter, spring, summer, fall, and thunderous rain,
The hard way of life gives me courage, conviction and character,
Which enable me to fight a raccoon and a wild boar's terror.
I am a Farm Girl.

Spring's turn tweak our chance.
Flowers' kiss and pairs dance.

Fire flies convene a party at dusk.
Frogs brag and seduce their love.
I am a Farm Girl.

I have my ambition and hobby.
Away from the village, I found my hubby.
So, we moved to a metro city.
Guess what was life? It is a pity.
I am a Farm Girl.

Every day three hours travel to and from the work place.
The dwelling was tiny and we lived in the constricted space.
There were few friends, but many activities.
Noise was creepy, nagging, and uncanny.
I am a Farm Girl.

I thought what a sheer waste of time!
My farms, animals and meadows are fine.
We are back; and enjoy our evening grill.
While kids swim in the creek and get a thrill.
I am a Farm Girl.

I am in the nineties and agile.
I hate at being reviled.
I walk five miles a day
That keeps the diseases at bay.
I have nine grandchildren.
My home, of which I am proud of, is a small kingdom.
I am a Farm Girl!

The Evening Train

It is a jam-packed evening train.
Wi-Fi waves jostle for space as do humans.
A small boy hangs around a pole and plays.
An advert reads: "Show Your Chivalry Now."
The train hosts passengers of diverse values.
They have varied outlooks from different milieu.
While in the train, to pass time, they are busy in personal zones.
Some read books and others murmur prayers for a job and a mortgage loan.

Some boys stare at beautiful faces and assets
As they depart, boys remorse with a loser's heart.
With headphones hooked in the ears,
Some follow the commentary of a soccer match.
They thrill as their favorite team scores a goal.

A girl shows empathy and kindness by helping an elderly man.
She vacates her seat for him to relax on the train.
The weather forecasts a mix of gales and heavy rain.
Fearing war in the gulf,
The Dow Jones Index loses value after some initial gains.

A loafer looking boy caresses a woman's bum.
She ignores him for avoiding trouble on the train.
A man sees this and tells her to teach him a lesson.
As accepting it will further prompt him to abuse and violations.
Gathering courage, she approaches the boy

She looks into his eyes without any fear and coy,
She spits on his face,
The boy tolerates the disgrace;
And he learns a lesson of life.

That evening the guard logs another incident of terror.
A lone woman faces a group of molesters.

As nobody comes forward to stop her predators, this adds fuel to the fire.
The criminals increase their grip of torture.
Sensing devils in their eyes, she makes her choice.
She decides to jump out of the running train and die to save her dignity and destiny.

A woman can fight back a single assailant,
But she cannot defeat a gang of predators on her own,
Unless those around help her to fight the attackers.

Pregnancy, Uterine Environment, and Embryonic Rights

The grandmothers advised expecting mothers to mind their gaits.
Eat healthy and well, grind some corn for porridge, but do not lift the heavy weights.
Nobody was able to know if the pregnant lady would gift a male child or female child.
It was full of suspense till the last moment, despite every parent longing for a male child.

The kings, to be blessed with a male progeny, performed rituals, rites, and even paid obeisance to saints.
Whether the heir would expand the boundaries of empire, though they desired, was not apparent.
The public followed the kings in their quest for a male child, and began aborting female fetus.
The sex ratio tilted in favor of boys, and this led to social evils like human trafficking, forced sex and rapes.

Juggernaut of Domestic Violence

For failing to bring enough dowry, a married woman is subjected to harsh punishment.
She is abused and suffers indignity in her own home at the hands of her own husband.
She is even forced to leave this world by her in laws and husband;
Nobody points a finger at them in the town.
Her story is covered by a mysterious shroud.

If she is unable to conceive after few years of marriage, this is a big problem for her.
She is humiliated if she gets a female child in the first séance.
A tremor of abuses erupts, if she gets several girls in quick succession.
Nobody blames her male partner for baby girls.
As if she alone is responsible for procreating babies.
She is obliged to silently accept all the taunts, insults, and even physical violence.
A counter argument by her is viewed as an indiscipline and crushed.

She is tortured for not able to give her family a male heir,
She does not fight back; she feels helpless as gets no support of her partner.
This ordeal is not her alone.
There are millions of women in the world,
Who like her are being crushed under the juggernaut of the domestic violence.

Cannot you assure a safe uterine environment?

An expectant mother is obliged to provide a safe uterine environment for her baby.

But things fall apart if the mother is an alcoholic, a smoker, a drug addict, or mentally ill.

The narcotics consumed by the expectant mother pollutes the uterine environment;
The drugs inflict an injury to the baby's growth; and
The baby is born with multiple health issues and disorders.

Caught by cops, the drug-addicted mother is sent to a correction facility.
No one is available to bring this baby up
As father has already separated from the woman.

The granny gets this child's custody,
The baby shines the granny's life at her sunset.
The moments they spend together are the happiest.

Rights of Embryos

The drug-addicted mother tramples on the right of an embryo to grow in the safe environment.
Though her conscience discourages her, temptations force her to not quit drugs keeping aside her child's development.
The embryo is unable to grow well in the womb of a drug-addicted mother.
 This strips the embryo of right to life.

Cruelty

She was an eighteen year old, on her way to home from college, was assaulted and raped.
The police arrested four beasts, but trivialized her story, and released them all on bail.

She protested the police, but they ridiculed her suffering and pain; and she drank the bile of their satire.
She poured petrol over her body with, lighted, and set herself and her humiliation on fire.

Why self-immolation?
Perhaps she thought:
The fire of self- immolation is colder than the fire of every day's social stigma and humiliation.
The flames of her fire will enlighten the spirit of society, saddled with inertia and notions of dark ages.
Her courage will raise the sagging morale of other men and women to rise, unite, and fight for justice.
Her bold actions will agitate cells of minds of legal luminaries to lambast the corrupt system and police.

The cruelty happens every day. Do we need a circumstantial evidence to prove it?
The cruelty is visible even to a blind eye in the women's abduction, rape and murder.
Despite a tough fight, they give in, to barbarism, to force, to fear; and they surrender.
The cruelty is in the men's mentality and they need to be corrected by the law to change the nature.
The cruelty is audible in the babbles of female fetus aborted; and in children's' cries amid fear of torture.

The graph of violence against women is rising; abounds in by many incidences of men's cruelty.
The imprints of it are recounted in folk tales, at the "ecological park" in the Mexico City.
The lords sell drugs to innocent minds in the city, even across borders, and amass fortune and wealth.
They rape and dump women, terrorize them, and women, as a result, are not able to freely breathe.

Thousands of women get killed every year, for their choice of her partner contrary to local traditions.
That smile was nothing but cruelty, after an "honor killing," to grind a fake and flimsy satisfaction.
Cruelty is in the man's mind, who promises to marry her later, rapes a young and beautiful woman,
Who will otherwise marry him in a normal situation, because the law condones that man's action?

The practice of "female genital mutilation," that disfigures the feminine dignity, has to end.
The women are to raise their voices and say the tradition that supports it, has to bend.
Health is wealth, and whatever comes in the way of a woman's health, has to mend.

Celebrating Women's Day!

Let them be what they wish to be,
If they like to be a model or perform in the public;
Or be a leader to serve the republic,
Or fly a fighter jet.
And let them cruise the ship of imaginations freely in the universe.
It does not make sense, at them, to yell
It is not an alarm bell
If they want to live life on their terms; and
If they want to choose their partner or profession.
Let them avail such opportunities that change their fortunes; and that make them an agent of change.
Let them run the race of their life, and try to win.

But they need moral and financial support; they need infrastructure to receive quality education; and they need empowerment, safety and security.

They need training and equipment to protect their dignity from the evil designs of predators or enemies.

War

My Oriental Lily: Peace

Here comes a little girl,
In her black and curly hair,
A five year old;
She is enthusiastic and bold;
Adventurous and gabby; and
She is intelligent, and sweaty:
She is my little Oriental Lily.
I hold her tight in my arms and lift her up in the air.
She is down to the floor, a few minutes after.
I asked Misha,
Could she lift me up?
Scratching her head, said, "She is too little to."
But if I could lighten myself, perhaps, when she is grown up, she would do.
I asked her, light like air?
"Yes," she said,
I wish I could become thin like air.
I could fly crossing over the distant borders.
I could help someone while he or she is skiing.
I could pull clouds to make rains in the parched lands.
I could whisper in the ears of those preparing to fight a war over the grass lands.
War is no solution.
Peace is forever.

Peace is the first and last option.
So, why should they not meet and discuss?
And stop the rhetoric and ruckus.

A Violinist in a War Zone

The habitants
Fear the bombs and violence,
And stay indoors in the eerie silence.

At far end of the city,
There is a gentleman awake.
In the ruins,
He is a violinist playing a tune,
In the honor of those vanquished in the civil war to observe a two minute silence.

Almost lying dead in the obscure corners;
Without uttering a word,
Heart beats rise
And they raise hands in total compliance.

But the machine guns begin fire;
And hand grenades are hurled.
The city faces fury, never before it is heard.
A feeble voice of heart whispers in her ears,
The road blocks?
She says, the love breaks them all;
And she moves forward.

Attired in a purple gown;
Towards the temple of love,
The Lady departs.

However, the Lady Luck chuckles!
A loud explosion in the city
Vanishes the infatuation;
And she runs for safety.
The splinters of desires fly crazy in the ruins.
'Do not fear the fear' now becomes the composer's tune.

In a makeshift theater, the silence acquires the center stage.
Nobody communicates the scripted dialogues.
Everybody uses symbols, gestures, and coded messages.
They do so to avoid a foe's fire, fury, and rage.

All of a sudden, the tune changes,
The "hatred cannot be pacified with hatred,"
The love is a pill that sweetens the hate.
But to expand the realm of love,
You ought to dispense hope to communities;
To men, women, the old, children and disabled; and to persons raped by devils.

Blessed by heavens,
The lady crosses the border,
And there she finds a shelter in a refugee camp.
She tries to sleep,
While praying in the dim light of an incandescent lamp for safety of her love,
But the fear and trauma don't let her sleep.
In the ruins, the violinist is left alone;
He is dejected and crestfallen.
In the camp,
The lady breaks down and pathetically cries.
After loosing the jewels of her eyes.

The Big Five

The king wolf ruled his community till he died in the jungle
His son received baton to rule the kingdom of the Jungle
As the community demanded rights to organize and speak,
He tortured them to repress their conscience and speech.
Repression, torture, and killings continue unabated
Innocent animals were regularly slaughtered.
Crimes were committed against the humanity by his state
Ruthless killings of citizens and children went to his credit.
All over the city were seen the disfigured faces, broken hearts, shattered hopes and lives.
Dead bodies scattered all around and coffins lined up for burial.

Pain filled the air and hands were raised for prayer.
There was nothing but pain to think, to breathe, and there were heard painful cries.
In the endless wait for dear ones to return home, better had hope and pray.
The worsening crises in the jungle gave a clarion call to the Big Five and all.
The Jungle's council convened a meeting to pass a resolution to extinguish the fast spreading fire.
Some voted for action; some absented; and others opposed the resolution.

There was no imminent solution; as the peace did not find a place in their Vision.
Meantime, the wolf perpetrated killings, torture; and mayhem.
The wolf wore a sheep's clothes and its conscience was dead,
He was unable to discern between good and bad.
Fear to lose the kingdom clouded his conscience; and he was sad.
His grief was uncalled for, as nobody lives in this world forever to rule or to be ruled.

Jungle's crises are man- made is a fact and it is very bad.
Therefore, the crises will not be resolved by God.
It can be resolved by the rule book of the jungle.
The Big Five should resolve crises by all means by being prudent and humble.
Without prejudice,
They should have collective vision, wisdom and a shared goal.
If they could delete strategic greed and selfishness from the equation, they would find a solution.

Misdemeanor

Everybody has a Silly Point!

Those who play cricket know very well about a "Silly Point" in the field. The "Silly Point" is a spot very close to the batsman. A fielder at this spot watches the moves of a batsman and tries to grab an opportunity to catch the ball and send him back to the pavilion. Generall speaking, there is a "Silly Point" for all of us in our respective fields.

A batsman knows that he has got a "Silly Point."
He is being watched by a fielder from a very close range at that point.
The fielder, being in the alert mode, tries to catch the ball that the batsman hits.
If the fielder does not drop the catch, the game for the batsman ends.
He is to return to the pavilion and sit.
Your game is your chance; if you win you will raise your neck high.
So don't let a person spoil it.
Everybody has a Silly Point!

The top notch players have their silly points in and out of the field.
They have the temptations for and are vulnerable to glamorous girls, gambling and greed.
Some of them indulge in the "match fixing" prompted by the temptations.
If they agree to lose,
They throw a "no-ball" or crawl instead of swiftly running.
One has to pay for an ignoble deed.
It is not a fun to play with the fire indeed.
Everybody has a Silly Point!

Some cricketers believe in tactics instead of skills to win the match.
They indulge in sledging, and hurling abuses at the opposing players.
They even temper balls;
As they are caught in things like these they suffer the worst humiliation of career.
It is impossible to recuperate a lost image and prestige, no matter what you do.
Everybody has a Silly Point!

A gentleman's Silly Point is his unassuming nature.
He readily accepts things and choices presented to him.
He rarely questions a motif or an agenda or the other person's intent.
His unassuming nature is often taken as gullibility,
The other persons manipulate
And take advantage of his unassuming nature.
No need to rush to decide in favor or against a deal.
Everybody has a Silly Point!

A CEO in his zeal to increase shareholders value has a big appetite for taking risk.
The rewards and returns to the shareholders up tick.

However, if the risky bet fails, shareholders lose money.
The firm files for bankruptcy,
The shareholders lose faith in his captaincy.
Everybody has a Silly Point!

A leader's "Kitchen Cabinet" disillusions other colleagues in the Cabinet.
She needs to watch her back from a hunter's tool;
And she has to do something to make hawks cool.
She should give to an unhappier lot a sheep with a coat of wool.
Everybody has a Silly Point!

A leader's addiction and lust for fair sex gets him into a trap laid by enemy's agents.
He is forced to quit power when he is caught; and the conviction tarnishes his image.
Having lost the face value, he is simply discounted.
His voice that was valued before in the official circles is no longer counted.
Lust for and addiction to sex takes one to the dead end.
Everybody has a Silly Point!

The priests and god men have substantial greed for wealth and lust for sex.
Some of them commit sexual abuses on boys and girls.
The children don't report to parents.
The media runs stories,
But parents prefer to remain silent
To not damage the reputation of a priest and institution or a god man.
Condoning a crime encourages criminals.
Everybody has a Silly Point!

A teacher disappoints pupils by muddling through in the class.
He or she should prepare and rehearse lessons before the class;

Make students enjoy the lessons like a cone of ice-cream after a brunch.
For not doing a thorough job, he or she becomes an object of satire to the class.
Everybody has a Silly Point!

The students postpone reading exercises to the rim.
But they spend nights to finish assignments to turn-in.
Manage your time strategically instead of doing nine credit hours in one go;
Bunching degrades performance, but you need good results to show.
Everybody has a Silly Point!

Procrastination

A man of the procrastinated mind, when he is asked to, says no to shake his body and bend.
And says no gain playing a sport, as both winners and losers return to the pavilion at the end.
A man of the procrastinated mind though he could, often tells he can't.
He doesn't mind indulgence in idle talks, gossips, gambling, and rant.

Anxieties run deep in mind, throat is dry, and the sea is always thirsty.
The thirst never dies, so a man of the procrastinated mind does not try to fetch water even for himself, and likes to remain thirsty.

Procrastination descends on mind like darkness during a solar eclipse.
When it comes to enjoying life, a man of the procrastinated mind likes an excuse.

The enthusiasm to improve his own life vanishes
When malicious thoughts blinds the conscience.
A man of the procrastinated mind does not like to learn from experiences of others.
He says, the experiences are sometimes joyous and other times nasty.
The outcome is not necessarily going to be desirable and tasty.
So a man of the procrastinated mind delays acting;
And he likes doing nothing. He has a silly point!

A man of the procrastinated mind therefore, harms his own goodness.
So why should we waste time in procrastinating;
And on things that we don't want.
We get it all,
But never do we get back a moment which is past.

Gossips

Sitting around the fire,
Guys tell stories about ghosts, mermaids, gins, and snake charmers.
About their blessings, curse, cure, revenge, and adventures.
Some indulge in the idle talks,
While others gossip about public figures, and politicians.
Talks touch on the social divisions, injustice; and corruption.
Which are headlines in a daily newspaper.
They are not rich but politically conscious and bread earners.
They are our country's proud citizens and voters.

People gossip about celebrities, and business tycoons.
When big names are sanctioned for misdeed like sex scandals,
Upon demand of justice by a victim,
The gossip mills churn new stories.
The famous names become objects of ridicule.
People like such stories of their downfall out of schadenfreude.

They all chew tobacco and spit saliva a little away from their shoes.
The fire does its job: while warming their bodies, it burns their woes.
Gossips entertain them:
A bit of socializing refreshes the moods.
The fire, friends, gossips and jokes fill the evenings in the rural milieu.
There is no night club; no reading room; and no indoor courts to play.
But people definitely urge to meet, and greet one another, and share worries.

Rumors-I (Females)

The rumors embellish gossips.
The rumors distort the image and reputation of persons who are rumored about;
The rumors humiliate, and isolate them.
Such persons avoid public places, and parks
Where they feel most insecure.
Their hearts sink; and the paces increase
As they pass through a group of hoodwinks.
Fearing social sanction and shame,
They don't share the turmoil with friends and family.
But by hiding an uncomfortable truth
They become vulnerable to a criminal's blackmail

Habitually who dodges the law, and escapes the terms of jail.

Rumors-II (Stampede)

Rumors that a bridge is collapsing turn an orderly crowd into a stampede;
People run helter-skelter to avoid getting crushed or killed.
In the commotion no one is insured.
Hundreds are dead, and injured in equal numbers due to stampede.
However, that rumor monger is never identified, and incarcerated.

Rumors III (Society)

Rumors abate intolerances against one another;
Rumors draw the communal lines in the society.
Rumors potentially change an ordinary incident to a communal flare up.
Initially spread through a mouth-to-mouth innuendo,
Soon, through social media, rumors reach out to hundreds of groups.
As these are transmitted back and forth
Between the groups.
A pure rumor is taken as the "fact."
That incites people to cause deadly tremors in the society.
The mobs lynch a man who it suspects of wrong doing.
The mobs rupture the Rule of Law,
And messages that leaders relay have inconsistencies and flaws.
The rumor mongering stokes a hateful fire in the society.
The communities do not shy of speaking ill and doing evil to one another.

The incidents of arson, looting, violence and losses of life do occur.
The vulnerable persons suffer.
The society is torn apart and the friendly relations go astray.
The suspicion in the minds of people stays.
They avoid to meet, greet, sale, purchase, and together celebrate.

Rumors IV (Business)

Though separated by thousands of miles, people connect instantaneously.
The internet offers them a free riding service, due to an inventor's chivalry.
The free riders misuse the assets .
The young people run websites for rumor-mongering; and
Publish spiced stories about names of fame: politicians and celebrities.
Tagged with commercials these attract eyeballs on the page and website.
Each click gets them some money,
Making money is everybody's dream,
But the money earned by means of the rumor-mongering is like a polluted stream.

Negative Emotions

Temptations

Jesus Christ delivered sermons to laity to not fall prey to temptations.
Did anybody follow him?
I do not know about man,
But definitely the mountains heard him,
They defeated the temptations.
And even today, they stand still and tall.
Unlike a convalescent person,
Who kills a man over a slight provocation in daylight?

The mortals are susceptible to the temptations.
Temptations deflect the attention even of a holy men away from God.
Lured by beauty, they allow their animal instinct; and run after sex and glamour.
They mix up the sex and divinity, and earn the shame.

The temptations run deep in the brains of mortals:
Their faculty is choked to think beyond a self-fulfilling greed.
The greed is a source of every problem be it injustice or crime.
The greed for wealth begets injustice to friends, neighbors, and even to unknown persons;
The greed for fair sex makes people cheat on spouses, friends and partners;
The greed for more profits makes merchants and contractors underpay for labor;
The greed leads public servants to corruption that infests the public life.
The greed leads to loss of integrity for a paltry sums,
People vend their character and country secrets.

Anger

There is anger in the air.

There is anger in the sea.
There is anger on the hills.
There is anger on the earth.

The anger is out on the street
It is so intense that it is unlikely to retreat.
The anger is spreading zigzag in all directions.
For anger, is there a reason and connection?

The anger is against leaders' inaction to address public grievances.
The anger is against their malfeasance and nonfeasance.
The anger is against the recalcitrant attitudes.
The anger is against human behavior that is rough and rude.

The environment in the city is smoggy and misty.
The drops of water dripping from her eyes is a pity.
Justice is unaffordable to her and a common man,
On–time justice is rare to an aggrieved woman.

The Obese Mind

The obese mind is tied with greed, anxiety, fear, anger, and evil in multiple chains.
 It is like a straw that is rotating in the whirlpool of emotions, and experiences a pain.
 Its weakness is its attachment to the pool and is afloat in the thunder and rain.
 The greed vitiates the mind with immoral tactics, in order to achieve a desired gain.
 The greedy mind catches an avoidable disease, depression, and contagious strains.

The greedy mind entraps an innocent soul on the internet and destroys a life.
The religions proscribe the greed, but a limit to greed, none of them prescribes.
The anxiety distracts a volatile mind, and vitiates thoughts amid swirling emotions.
A guru tricks a worrisome man to pray to off-load his worries and burdens.
The anxiety weakens and makes mind susceptible to an emotional loot and ransom.
The worries deprive a man from enjoying good foods, music, and colors of the spring blossoms.

The obese mind drifts towards an evil as the obesity enters in an irreparable phase.
The shadows act diabolically and vitiate landscape with violence and blaze.
Evil deeds instill fear in minds and kill dreams that people would want to chase.
But the courage of conviction deflects fear, and a flight takes-off, despite an irrational haze.

The obese mind is fearful to lose what it has inherited from past generations.
The fear of losing face worries an obese mind, and he is always on the run.
The obese mind is a slave of whims and is volatile, like a lump of Sodium.
The anger blankets the mind and the obese mind loses the internal equilibrium.

Peace does not visit naturally to the obese mind, but the violent tendencies return back.
If mind is light, it is free of greed and fear- the locomotive of life runs on a right track.
Then, mind flies like a sparrow, and enjoys a dive in the universe.

The eternity of hope displaces bouts of depression and hopelessness,
Just as the rising sun darkness.

Ethos

Inspired by ethos
Kings relinquished empires and set up tiny cottages at the banks of the river.
Minimized the needs, and abandoned the lust and greed.
They lived in solitude, and silence.
And by helping an helpless man,
They got an immense satisfaction.
They burnt the ego, while living on the riverbank in this fashion.
Their needs were minimal.
They invented a technology to know and control the self.
And what the nature revealed, they recorded in the books.
Their selflessness, as merged with the community interest,
helped them win friends and followers.

The poor romanticized their love to God.
Their means were simple, and uncorrupt.
Highly revered ones were saints of medieval times.
Their words are still sung.
Their names are still eulogized.
And their image is clean without a speck of dust or dent.

Their advice:
Let the mind be tranquil;
Let it be eager to acquire virtues and loathsome to vice.
Let it eject junk ideas.

Let it reject the dead cells from the body;
Let it rejuvenate the aged cells; and
And let it live in silence and solitude as much as possible in harmony with nature.

Society

These People Need to Pause!

The single parents or working couples, give cons to their kids, instead of time. The tender minds live in the surreal world unless they hear an inspiring story and rhyme. These people need to pause!

Now-a-days, kids and teenagers watch cartoon films and play video games. For hours, they remain absorbed in the dream world, while parents forget their responsibility and aim. These people need to pause!

The uncontrolled internet surfing makes the teenagers superficially euphoric. Like when not getting a dose of drug an addict becomes restless, teenagers are apathetic. These people need to pause!

The young people use drugs and consume alcohol to ward-off the worries and tensions. The narcotics and hard drinks flip them to float freely in the air, but do these things entertain? These people need to pause!

The addiction to drugs, alcohol, online chatting, dating, and consenting to making the love, lead to unwanted pregnancies, gambling, theft, violence, while parents get a wrong side rub. These people need to pause!

Not knowing how to fix, young people mentally suffer from a humiliating loss. They neither show interest in the game of life, nor in choosing a chance like a choice of head or tail at a coin's toss. These people need to pause!

Being disinterested in the work or study, and to their existence the negativity swirls. In this hell, it seems they will pass entire life, unless there is a miraculous idea. These people need to pause!

Viewing the rising sun effectively destroys darkness even inside a shroud. The sun radiates hope, while the moon enlightens the persona to stand out in the crowd. These people need to pause!

Listening to an inspirational music writes- off the depressing thoughts. There exists opportunities to cleanse the stains and blots in life. These people need to pause!

There is no way to rejuvenate the jaded cells in the mind without the hope and will power. They need to make efforts to switch on the dynamo of their willpower. These people need to pause!

Identities clash

The communities differentiate one another, on the basis of caste, religion and race.
The interfaith romance is forbidden but the disharmony and hatred grow like wheat tares.
The self-styled leaders fire emotions in the name of religion, and influence people's conduct.

The followers don't question them, and such leaders turn egotists and even autocrats.

Caste

The caste based groups,
Demand job reservations in the government sector and protest.
So called, the peaceful marches are intrinsically violent.
The protesters create chaos on the street:
They attack bikes and buses which cross their path
The radical elements damage and burn private and public properties.

The schools are closed;
The businesses are forced to shut down.
The national highways witness the traffic jam.
The weary passengers stranded in the Lorries groan.
Small children moan.
They harass, molest, and even rape a woman who unfortunately, lands herself in the hot waters.
The protesters even deny a passage to an ambulance to the hospital despite its honks.
The patient leaves this world on the way to the hospital.
But the protesters continue to agitate; and they clash with government agencies.
They don't leave the site.
The law enforcing agencies mutely spectate;
And the government fails in the governance test.
Everybody is made to pay
For public assets that agitators burnt and damaged.
I ask this question,
Are these agitators' victims of social injustice?

Religion

The politicians don't believe much in it, but exploit it to their advantage.

They instigate fights between people; and different groups build their dominions.
The politicians use rhetoric to whip up religious emotions,
The society polarizes along the religious lines; and is split.
The virtual dividers separate the suspicious communities, along the religious and racial lines.
Fear-stricken communities live in groups, and the fear forbids them to display any identity based signs.

What runs deep in the human psyche is suspicion and lack of trust between communities.
There is a need to remove the mistrust as soon as possible to the hilt.
The vote bank politics likes the status quo to continue.
Nobody knows how long would the mistrust go?

No one thinks about and takes an in-depth journey to the spiritual universe.
The old order, rituals, and dogmatism become insignias of faiths, however.
The symbols and robes décor the men and women,
The outward appearances steal the show; it is common
While real intents hide behind the garbs and robes.
People pride in the obscurantism, old order, and discriminatory practices
Against persons of the other faith; the twisted lips hide hatred and prejudices.
Religious intolerances obstruct the road to shared living, celebration, and prosperity.
Religious intolerances are an earthly reality.

Race

I overheard these words:
They are dogs; I hate them.

How could a person born with dark, brown, or yellow skin, be inferior to a white skin person?
How could anyone acquire a license to hate a person for his skin color?
How could a person judge another person on the basis of the color of his skin?
The notions of dislike and disapproval are inbuilt in a person's consciousness, and create a maze of biases.
Which leads such a person to feel superior, and can incite him to be violent and abusive, even though there is no provocation.
The social harmony becomes an easy prey due to capricious and hateful behavior.
To do everything to seek approval and liking of such a person is not called for,
As whatever you do is not going to erase prejudices, biases, and notions from their memoir.
So don't ever try!

The Vote Bank

The identity gives a name to a community which support en masse a leader who identifies with them and their community
Which does not betray the leader in any circumstance, and in whose safe hands the community entrusts its future, hope, aspirations, and prosperity.
The bonds of the identity cement the trust between the community and the leader, and vice versa.
The community is a Vote Bank for the leader, who for his electoral campaign, draws support from the community,
Which fully participates and involves in the campaign financially and morally to galvanize general public support for its leader's victory.

Campaign Money

Politicians get money to contest elections from the vote banks, money launderers, external sources, businesses and industries.
They control police and manipulate the law, due to loopholes, and blame external hands for every single crisis.
They put their family interests above all; and their discourse on the country's welfare is meant for public consumption and publicity.
They mislead the public by their rhetoric and repeat a lie until the public perceives that as a fact in an anxious city.

Elites

The leaders are elites in the political context hobnobbing with police and bureaucracy, expanding their wealth and popularity. Facilitated by the age old system, nexus is established between the police, political elites, delinquents and bullies.
Masking real designs, they show a compassionate face to trick public and establish credibility and their political worth.
The wealth expands the political sway, which gets them more power, and with the increased power comes more and more wealth.

Bullies support them in the political pursuits.
In the vote bank politics, the wealth and the bullies matter.
The confluence of the three takes their political fortunes to new heights.
The organization and the government give them an influential berth.
A leader cannot succeed in the political arena without the vote bank, wealth and bullies.
The identity overrides all of the above, and helps rally public support behind him.
A poor citizen cannot cultivate the same political fortunes, as they lack in the means and ways.

As folk tales say, poor people sitting at the fringes of democracy, are overshadowed by the elites.

Bullies

Politicians domesticate the bullies whose job is to bully persons making noise at the command of leaders.
If the leader is implicated in a crime, the bully goes to jail with or in place of his dear leader.
Bullies are ready to die for their leader; and they bark like a dog does on an intruder, for his master.
They disregard the rule of law, risking their lives for the service of their master.

Bullies believe that the master is a real benefactor and savior, and will always rescue them.
However, politicians dump a bully if he becomes a liability and is of little or no value to them.
Bullies commit crimes at the behest of masters, thinking that public will never know and react.
Politicians deploy bullies to frighten and even kill journalists who expose their criminal acts.

Law

Politicians love the laws that are vague and silent about the conflict of interest and transactions of quid pro quo type.
They establish new companies, embezzle shares and purchase properties to live, show off, and contest elections.

The media debates the sacking of such politicians; and leaders do not like overhauling institutions to end these malpractices forever.
The public want laws that would punish such politicians for corruption in the conflict of interest situation.

In the din of accusations and counter accusations, a chance to fix a legal inefficiency is lost.
The confrontation wastes the time and public is miffed; and to the society the political quarrels cost a lot.
Being confused, public does not see a "light at the end of the tunnel," and hope is bitten by the frost.
Without a dialogue, it is impossible to harmonize the opposing views of main protagonists.

Elite Culture

The elite culture is about the branding of privileges and immunity unavailable to common man.
The vulgar display of these symbols in the public space, causes everyone much discomfort and pain.
They threaten the law enforcing authorities and apply their own rules to create social tensions.
Traffic is blocked; even an ambulance is stranded to let an elite caravan pass through a junction.
Elite progeny unauthorized assume privileges without any official sanction, and interfere in the affairs of the state.
With that delusion, they perpetrate instances of social injustices, and cause victims to fear and frustrate.
The elites use the political influence to jump a queue of scarce economic opportunities.
They are not entitled to a quota. They win a contract without an auction, to service a war-torn city.

Bullies jump a queue and hurt the sentiments of people behind them that gentlemen ignore.
But a person whose protest is battered, goes into a coma, and lives in this world no more.

The Post-Truth Life

The truth is a virtue, and eternal is the truth. But now in the post-truth era, it can be cultured like artificial pearls. If it is spoken a hundred times before an audience which is amenable to an emotional rhetoric, the cultured truth or half-truth will be perceived credible. Wow, a sin is convertible into a virtue!

Is violent protest by mob effectual? Are those marchers shouting in vain? Perceptibly, there is a lot of anger in the atmosphere. Can the anger be dissipated by a fan?

The lines drawn on the sand can be erased by a dust storm. But what about the fault lines between the civilizations? Who can blur them? Can the intolerances across faiths be buried alive?

People are haunted by an apocalyptic scene that might be unleashed by a possible nuclear war or terror. Can the abettors of terror be tamed? Can the unholy intents be quashed by cosmic rains?

The Temple Trust is in Breach of Trust

It is dusk time,
The stillness sets in the atmosphere.
A senior priest conducts rituals to the evening prayers.
The bell rings; the priest lights camphor; and shows lamps to goddess.
The devotees join the priest, and sing songs to praise and please the goddess.
She blesses everyone.
But none has an inkling about what is going to happen.

The night swings in action;
Everybody retires to relieve from the tension.
The queen of night is restless in her mansion.
Conniving with pigs,
Elephants organized a display of fireworks to scare away the evil forces.
The goddess of death watched their crookedness from her fortress.

The elephants lit the fireworks. The sparks felled on warehouses which stored a lot more fireworks which were also ignited.
All around there were multiple explosions with terrifying sounds, and flying rocks.
The rocks and fireballs hit the viewers
The fear stricken folks ran in ten directions to avoid being killed.
With teary eyes, they ran into and over one another.
The melee mutilated the face of hope in the temple premises.
Over a hundred persons were killed.
Mingled with fear and grief, throats were choked.
This tragedy triggered a mutiny by public
against the pigs and elephants for continuing the phony rituals.
Next day, the media ran a story in gory detail.
The pigs blamed the elephants; and the elephants the pigs.
The elephants went to hide, while the pigs suggested to carry out an institutional rejig.

The time never stops: It heals the losses, scars and wounds.
After a hiatus of seven days, the temple doors were opened for public to come and pray.
The politicians discussed the tragedy, while the public cursed the temple trustees,
For they ignored a government ban to light fireworks and display;
 And compromised the public safety.

Note: Pigs symbolically represent local politicians; and elephants the temple trustees.

Self-Styled God Men

He heads a cult organization and commands thousands of followers.
The worth of every god man is millions of dollars.
What do they use the wealth for?
Well, the wealth takes them close to the center of power.
The wealth and power like a Siamese twin coexist.
Together they control the destiny and business of the country.

The god men become famous.
As people worship the rising sun.
In the favorable time, a graph of their fame rises
Like the Dow Jones Index.
However, their fortunes nosedive to shame,
When they are convicted for questionable deeds and religious practices.
Like sexual abuse of young girls and child sacrifices.
Their empires crumble;
Their ambitions derail; and
Their reputation and image in the public eyes fall.
However, the wealth that they accumulated just changes hands.

Like a gift from father to a daughter, and from daughter to father, and so on.

Is the wealth of god men taxable?

The Old Man and the Queue

I was in a queue to pay my electricity bill;
The queue was a long curve of many Jack and Jill.
An old man came, breathing long and fast;
He didn't want to be at the end and last.
He, somehow, inserted his body in the line;
He had a stick to support his spine.

A man asked him, when he saw so may bills in his hands:
"Have you brought bills to pay on behalf of your neighbors also?"
He said "no"; he continued: "his sons."
And he began to cry; and tears rolled down the cheeks from his eyes.

The tears narrated his agony and pain;
He said, "For him, the old age is like an engine of an aging van"
His life is experiencing bouts of cloudy winter and rain;
But blaming anybody is vain.
The emotional support he used to get from the sons is waning;
And he is too old to acquire a new skill and training.

The man behind counseled: The old age is an age-old reality.
We should treat it in entire civility."
The rich pay bills of elderly folks in the old homes;

But unable to afford, the poor let their elders hit the rock.
The bonds of blood in the old age crumble;
The intestines too often rumble;
And seniors expect us to them to be nice and humble.

Corruption

Unlike a little cash offered obliges a temple deity, a bribe obliges everybody in the systematic loop.
A bribe is shared by one and all; by everybody from bottom to top; as a result a boss does not sanction subordinates; peers do not complain about, and clerks do not gossip during the tea break in the cafeteria.

The corruption has infested the human organs and institutions, and outliers are branded as fools, who even their spouses ridicule.
They flaunt wealth, the corrupt persons legalize the stealth through buying land, fancy jewelry, and big vehicles.

When the demonetization came, the hoarders deceitfully converted their black money into white.
In connivance with bank staff who received kickbacks; who succumbed to their influence and might.

Corruption breeds the corrupted individuals; and corrupt practices:
And the corrupt practices grow like branches and roots of a banyan tree.
Below which the probity dies an unnatural death,
But the shameless shoots multiply under the same tree.

Corruption is also about having the identity based sensibilities in the republic.
The public rallies behind a convicted leader of their community;

They pressurize the state to get him unhooked when he is booked by the law enforcement agencies.

The corruption is a tumor which everybody across party lines agree, but no consensus to eradicate it.
The corruption is an inconvenient truth which our society conveniently accepts. Without bribery the files don't move; justice is not dispensed; and mothers are forced to give birth to babies on the floor of a hospital.

The corruption is rampant in the police, electric utilities, banks, public schools, hospitals, and in the rest.
The common man under duress pays bribes to cops, bankers, technicians, bureaucrats and to the rest.
The corruption being systematic, becomes worse if the unethical leadership sits at the top.

The corruption will not go away until the nexus is broken between politicians, criminals, contractors, bureaucrats and cops.

The corruption will continue until the public elects leaders who will withstand all pressures and never flop.
Only carefully selected or elected leaders break the nexuses and free the soul of a country from corruption.
Top leaders which have business interests should refrain from leading government or an organization.
The leaders with conflict of interest could easily tweak public policies to facilitate businesses and organizations, and influence individuals and aliens.

Bad Cops, Good Cops

The cops are human beings like us.
The virtues and vices make them good or bad.
Leaders influence their style and approach to job. .

Good leaders watch their conduct.
And allow them do their job without fear.

Good cops during the civil strife maintain the peace;
enforce the rule of law that ensures public safety.
People are able to stroll, walk fearlessly in the evening after the dinner.
Good cops rescue people when they are in distress.
They rescue a woman groped by bandits trying to snatch her necklace.
They promptly take an injured man to the hospital, for medical caress.
They make sure that a kidnapped baby returns home safely;
 And the hijacked car to the rightful owner.
Good cops stand straight in the wake of pressures and political insinuations.
Their actions conforming to the rule of law, favor none and are prejudicial to none.
Good cops are kind hearted: treat everyone equal before the law.
In difficult situations they don't lose sense of humor; their devotion to duty knows no flaw.
They earn the public trust as people believe in their professionalism and integrity.
God cops alleviate fear by giving the public a higher sense of security.
The public appreciate their sacrifices, and dedication to service and duty.
And what good cops like to treasure in memory is the public recognition of their service and duty.

Bad cops on the other hand, influenced by extraneous factors,
implicate an innocent person, while they are lenient with a

culprit.
They reluctantly hear the problems of voiceless and poor.

Bad cops prejudge an individual based on his race, caste, identity, and religion.
When a victim succumbs to their misjudgment chaotic protests ensue, and tarnish their image.

Cops who patronize criminals are bad; they together instill fear in the public psyche.
As law and order deteriorate, the public cry foul, but the vested interests gain from the crises.

Misguided by their animal instinct, bad cops criminally abuse a trafficked woman.
And they exploit her vulnerabilities for sensual pleasures, but when they are caught droop like a dog.
Bad cops do not place value to the rule of law;
Their actions are modulated by bribes and kickbacks.
They will go on as long as the systematic vices prevail.
But as virtuous leaders emerge in the system, the corrupt cops suffer humiliation and setback.

Global Threats

Inequalities

The increasing gap between the elites and the poor does not bode well for social harmony.
Increasing temperatures and terrorism are set to exacerbate the social tensions and acrimonious acts.
Uncertain times wrinkle the spirit of hope. Anxieties and worries don't let us cope.
Elites must build castles of hope;
And refrain from the inward looking policies, and motives demanding more and more.

Poverty

In a public restaurant, when a poor person grabs a portion of a leftover fish to fill his belly,
The poverty manifests in terms of the lost human dignity.
When a mother sells her dear child to human traffickers to pay debts, not because she is greedy,
Poverty manifests in hopelessness and helplessness through the distressed sale of an asset of last resort.
When a person is forced to work in the bonded circumstances, in sheer silence,
Poverty manifests in the voicelessness and complete surrender to torture and violence.
When a leader does not recognize women as an economic agent of social change,
Poverty manifests in human prejudices, stereotypes against women, and ignorance.
When a culture does not treat women at par with men,
Poverty manifests in terms of aborted female fetuses, human trafficking, rapes and violence.
When a culture treats women as mere sneakers on men's feet,
Poverty manifests in terms of domestic violence, and unhappy family.
Poverty persists because there is poverty of ideas;

Poverty persists because human dignity, as a value, is not treated at par with other values.
Poverty persists because so many needy, underprivileged, and undernourished people remain to nurture.
Poverty persists because leaders lack conviction to challenge the patriarchic mindset of men against women.
Poverty persists because of scornful attitudes of the rich toward the poor.

Immigrants

The Irish famine struck;
And people fled homes;
They sailed; and reached the American shore.
The stories of the struggle are found in the folklore.

Nowadays the men and women from the poor countries do the same.
They sell their farms and silver to journey to Europe to set up a new home,
And taste meat balls on rye bread with wine and cheese.
Green things please the eyes!
They try to cross the ocean, with the help of a trafficker,
The guy overloads the boat.
The risk to every passenger increases is the upshot.
The overcrowded boat, the rough sea and the wild waves cause panic and commotion.
In intense prayer and meditation, the heads bow down.
The boat continues to sail.
The sea sicknesses grip everybody.
The passengers are exhausted and ill.

The fury of the sea douses the fire of intense prayers.
For having overloaded the boat, everyone curses the trafficker.
The engines begin to fail.
Passengers screeches in fright;

By tooth and nail the death they fight.
The alarm bells ring.
The boat finally sinks.
The coast guards rescue those who are lucky.
The stars in the cosmos watch the tragedy.

In this episode,
None, but the greed is a winner.
The greed, however, generates vices.
The greed vitiates human choices.
The greed causes injustice to passengers and society.

Refugees

The war has rewritten destiny, and forced millions of people to run away from tyranny.
To safer places to avoid the persecution, torture and agony.
None but a few nations embrace them;
Show compassion and empathy to refugees.
While the rest of countries blow cold and hot.
Can these hapless people be simply bowled out without a chance to play a shot?
The war is at its peak, and millions of refugees spend sleepless nights in inhumane conditions.
Having no hearth to warm up, they invoke faith to generate heat to bear cold and adapt to these conditions.
Lucky enough would they be if they could find a safe shelter, food and medicines to avoid loss of life and deprivation.

Nuclear War

The earth is replete with smog, pollution, terrorists, violence, and lusty sharks.
The deficiency of love to humankind is stark.
The stars are far away, and friends are not around to chat.
After good fielding; it is now the time to bat.

The missile-loaded launchers are ready to fire.
The war may begin by a trigger-happy solder's ire.
The fear of a nuclear war in the world is real.
The challenges of the global peace are not trivial.
The threats of nuclear war are genuine.
The leaders and devils are making a union.

Water War

Similar to what makes people riot at a water point in the water thirsty world,
Nations too can go to war for control over the rivers, lakes, and seas, and assert the right.
The threats of war loom large over the control of sea routes, and shared water resources.
As mighty nations want to control the exploitation of energy and minerals under the sea; and
As the riparian nations in the upper reaches force the river to change the course.

Religious Intolerance

You accuse him for apostasy just because
He studies other scriptures to know how people seek God in other faiths.
Does it make sense?

You accuse him for apostasy just because
He wants to prepare a platform of shared human values:
Love, freedom, respect for human dignity, peace and harmony.
Is this harmful to you?

You accuse him for apostasy just because

He wants to establish an adjustable, an adaptive; and an accommodative contract for shared prosperity between various faiths based on shared understanding of human values.
Does it make sense?

You accuse him for apostasy because
You dislike him making roads in other faiths
Which you fear will inspire others to tread on those roads.
With your iron hand, you can curb these aspirations,
But a high probability of a high tide against the mental slavery cannot be eliminated.

You accuse him for apostasy
Because you mistake his earnest desire to learn aout other faiths is a precursor to a demand of religious freedom
Which you despise as it poses a threat to your existence and your future is at stake.
Your fear may be valid, but your judgement does not make sense.

So you execute him for a demand of religious freedom, which is untrue.
But it is your insinuation for his enquiry.
You eliminate a foe,
Though he is your own real brother, and a sibling.
Your action sows a seed of mistrust between religious communities
Which live in silos.
You change the course of history for bad for which future generations will never forgive you.
Didn't you commit a crime against humanity?

Terror

Terror is a threat to global peace and security.

Breeding Fields of Terror

Where people have the "holier than thou" attitude,
The darkness pollutes the rectitude.
Minds eject the rational thoughts.
And in the midst of crisis they are caught.
The perspective of life is damaged.
These are breeding fields of terror.

Where religious symbols are held in high esteem,
Virtues and values run out of steam.
Drenched in the filth of bigotry,
The identities clash; violence erupts after the simmering social tension.
The public bears the brunt; and the public curses the leaders for the situation.
These are breeding fields of terror.

Where waves of the negativity merge with radio waves in the atmosphere.
It hits minds, markets, soldiers, owners, servants, and even neighbors across the border.
It is also dispensed as a free dose in daily sermons, and shapes young people into devilish characters.
These are breeding fields of terror.

The terror infested minds don't like people enjoy and celebrate.

The terror infested minds decide about people, based on their skin color, that they are non-believers.
The terror infested minds mow down innocent persons reveling in a country.
The terror infested minds mow down innocent persons biking in a country side.
Is getting killed in this manner their destiny?
These are breeding fields of terror.

The Phalanx of Negative Minds

Violence, vice, prejudice, greed, and conspiracies are weapons of the phalanx of negative minds
Being strong like a hurricane, they damage the opposing barriers and structures and blind everybody that comes in the range.

Never rest in peace, violent minds pick fights, and goad others to violence, in their net.
They don't value their own life and after killing others, they show no remorse or no regret.

Loaded with vice, negative minds traffic human beings, and force them into bonded labor and prostitution.
A word of wisdom, even from God, may not convince them to reverse their positions.

The negative minds whirl under the influence of powerful religious and sectarian torques.
Preconceived notions give them the fire power to burn schools, temples and mosques.

The negative minds proclaim the invincibility of the phalanx on the turf of wide spread negativity.

One hopes one day their empire will crumble when defeated by the forces of rationality.

Silence Screeches in Pain

Dhamaal is performed by devotees in Sufi Shrines These people seek to communicate directly with God. However, their way of seeking God is not liked by the extremists. They exploded a bomb which killed over 100 people inside a shrine.

God is known for His omnipotence, omniscience, and omnipresence.
God is a source of eternal fragrance that permeates the space in ten directions.
God is unconditionally compassionate towards us.
God is a source of an effulgent light
That dispels our ignorance and evil thoughts.

The love-drenched souls swirl to that light
Like a moth encircles a lamp.
They are dancing Dervish;
They love God intensely.
The heat of the love burns the temptations that are earthly.

They hope and desire to hear the "Kun" (be)
The sound appeared at the time of creation.
They want to communicate with Him directly
To untie knots of religious pedagogy, extremism, and hypocrisy.

They tread on the traditions of syncretism.
However, puritanical harangues do not like their ideas
To build bridges
Between cultures divided by a schism.
The puritanical harangues want the dance to end.

As the hatred reached its pinnacle,
The extremists exploded a bomb within the shrine.
That killed over a hundred people, and injured dozens.
The blast shattered peace –the pride of the shrine
Built by bricks of love and mortar of tolerance.

The silence screeched in pain.
The white paints on the walls got the red blood stains.
However the alacrity remains alive.
Dhamaal that the religious harangues criticize, resumes and thrives
But they condone the terror and violence. Why?

Cruelty of Time versus Terror

Time

So what? Time was or is cruel to you.
Thank the sun, and the sea, for splendid views.

If the time's cruelty stunts your imagination, mission, and the power of will.
Assume the control of yourself, rise from ashes, and climb the hill.

Standing on the hill, speak your mastery and mind to thousands of fellow folks.
Inspire those, who are dying of time's cruelty, depression, drugs, and heart strokes.

It is true that the happiness lies in the liberty, without which our throat and voice choke.
People enjoy freedom if they get real things, not like promises which vanish like smoke.

The lust for power debauches the canvas of public policy.
The rhetoric or narratives are seldom free from the fallacy.
Time's cruelty reduces the shine, but a rising sun clears the fog.
Hope stimulates positive action;
Unconditional love breaks the block of hate.

Terror

Terror's cruelty cuts short innocent lives and deprives them of their dreams.
The new ways to strike, make the intelligence men groan and people scream.

Terrorists hate festivity, occasions of joy in society, and celebrations.
They hate freedom, and strike at will, and gain strength in a civil strife situation.

Stock prices slide; commodities sales weaken; and moods are sad and somber.
The unfolding crises kicks the sell-off; and equities worry about an uncertain future.

Inspired by cultural biases, monsters of hate thrive, though their crimes are terrible.
Can you kill devils by a few rituals like throwing at devils a few pebbles?

The cruelty caused by terror shatters hope, aspirations and friendships everywhere.
The old dictum reminds us to "watch your back and keep open your eyes and ear."

The cruelty of terror inflicts heavy casualties in the city and people groan under the debris of permanent loss.
They remember the good time spent with the loved ones, but future holds no hope.

Hate

Hate is deceptive. It is there, but
It appears like an iceberg, which hides mostly in the water, but its tip is exposed.
The berg tricks an unassuming sailor, whose ship unknowingly hits the berg and wrecks.
People sell it in the name of religion;
People buy it in the name of religion.
The buyers and sellers collude,
They kill anybody for no sin, in the name of religion.
The market for hate is expanding;
The sellers of hate are increasing;
The buyers of hate are multiplying
Because the value of human life is fast declining.
The market of religious intolerance is bullish.
The investors of sin are upbeat.

Liabilities of Hate

Many children lose parents killed in the terror infested violence.
Many children lose parents killed in the sectarian violence.
Many children lose parents killed in the chemical warfare.
Many children lose parents killed in the civil war.
Many children lose parents in the child trafficking.
Many children lose parents in the communal violence.

The children without parents are liabilities.

The liabilities of hate are increasing,
However, the assets of goodwill are shrinking;
The goodwill is real cash at the till.
We have to erase the liabilities of hate, and multiply the assets of goodwill.
Is there another solution of this puzzle?

Fear

The Demon of Fear – Part I

Life for all of us, in one way or the other, is full of fear.
It is loss of something which is near and dear.
You can kill the fear; so why not try!
It has no odor; it is colorless.
To talk about it is not pointless.
It is unreal but it appears in the memory.
It is the basis of many fearful stories.

Vested interests use it as a weapon.
They create an image of a demon.
They use it to grind their own axe.
So it is good to do something about this to fix the problem.

They create fear with terror and violence;
And prevent girls to get education.
One of them, Malala, raises her voice.
But she pays a heavy price.

The constant fear haunts females in the metro cities' roads and rails.
That they may be attacked or raped
The law is toothless to defend their honor; it sets a criminal free on bail

Citing lack of evidence as a reason.

Due to fear that persists in their mind,
They make choices stupid and unkind.
Females abort a female foetus before it is born!
They perhaps do not mourn.

It is the fear that makes them shut their doors.
Opening the heart is what they abhor.
They have static and rigid minds;
And infected by a virus of unusual kind.

The Demon of Fear - Part II

The fear is an emotional turmoil
The fear of an unfamiliar turf daunts us all
The fear's mold prejudices our mind;
It spreads its contour unless it is made to rescind.

To insure against fear, some people kneel in a mosque;
And some kneel by the temple wall.
Some people raise hands up in the sky.
Others orient their minds to deep inside.

But the fear keeps bouncing back into our psyche.
In Delhi's chaotic traffic, it is the feeling when you bike.
It is the feeling when your plane's landing gear is stuck.
A choice between "a devil and deep blue sea" frustrates.

Who Fears None?

Most of us fear the unknown, but persons of courage and conviction, fear none.
All living beings fear limits on life, but the time fears none.
Clouds fear blistering sun;
River fears pollution;
Nature fears human greed; and
Wildlife fear shadows and greedy men.
Valleys fear landslides;
Grass fear hooves of elephants.
But the ocean fears none; and
The heights fear none.
Most of us fear the failure, but daredevils and passionate hearts fear none.
Darkness fears light; bats fear the day, but an enlightened soul fears none.
A maltreated woman fears everyone, but an empowered woman fears none.
A pampered child fears nightmares, but a child who is trained to fight the fear, fears none.
A corrupt leader fears everyone, but a man of integrity and letters, fears none.
A wavering mind fears loneliness, but a steady mind fears none.
Cowards fear the defeat, but the lionhearted men and women fear none.
Traitors fear death, but a patriot soldier earns fame, and fears none.

Men, Rivers, and Seas

By the River Narmada

The Narmada is revered as goddess by the countless devotees.
Clearing the dirt that stains their soul is her divine duty.
The goddess rides on a crocodile
That displays her friendship with and love for biodiversity.

It is a common belief
That her waters solidify bones, and her view ends mental strife.
Of the three earthly sufferings her grace frees a miserable life.
So they dip their bodies in the holy waters.
And get what they plead as the Narmada is a kind giver.

Her grace removes the penury of human vision.
Her grace equalizes the opportunities given to a king and commons.
It is said, even though one is naive,
By camping at the bank of the Narmada, he or she becomes wiser.
So they camp and meditate;
And give up illusion, animal instinct, and even silver.
She benedicts them
Filling their consciousness with peace and pleasure.

The diehard devotees circumambulate the sacred River,
And during the journey they view the"Amarkantak," the source of Narmada, and waterfalls,
And the sun shines the hills, lush green fields, temples, birds, and wildlife, and the road side stalls.
The road side vendors sell some exotic fruits and herbs,
Which cures even an incurable disease.
These herbs also dissipate their physical and mental fatigue.
But men are essentially ungrateful to the Narmada.
They are bent upon destroying natural habitats, shrubs, and cutting trees
Through mining minerals satisfying the insatiable greed.
All of which exasperate the climate's ferocity;

All of which shake the River's resolve to forever serve the humanity.
Could we reverse the perils of human folly?

The Ganges is sick and unhappy

Hearing bells that ring in the hearts,
Hordes of people walk to the River Ganges to bathe in the holy waters.
The Ganges is their goddess;
She gives them shelter, and removes their sufferings.
The water that was once upon a time milky, now looks muddy.
They fear,
As they wade in the water,
Little by little
The fear goes away;
They exclaim,
The River is shallow!
Where has the water gone?
Has it been stolen?
In the midst of the river,
They repeat sacred hymns, as they dip and dive.
Some people swim.
While some of them exercise to trim their bellies.
They take selfies to capture and archive every moment.
Marigold flowers, burnt charcoal pieces, and ashes
arrive, floating on the water.
The rituals that people shore up
Knowingly or unknowingly,
Contaminate the Ganges.
The water becomes unfit for human use, but people refuse not to use it.
Their faith in the Ganges is unshakable: that water of the Ganges will purify their bodies and souls.
I see a woman fill a bottle with water and drink it whole;

She suffers from dysentery and diarrhea,
Others also fall sick due after they consume the polluted water.
Shouldn't someone somehow warn people to not consume the water at specific spots?
It is an irony that those of us who revere the Ganges most, pollute the River and make it sick.
Her soul is injured and she is unhappy.
She does not wish to continue to flow in disrepute as a polluted river.
People who revere her should accord the River status and dignity by respecting her wish, and not pollute her waters.
They need to change their behavior and redefine their relationship with her in order to make the Ganges happy.
They need to restore her image and give her the sanctity she had at the beginning of civilization.

The Nile is Sad

The violence in Egypt makes the Nile sad. The anatomy of incidents suggests that the" reasonableness" was the most conspicuously absent in both sides of the equation.

The papyruses are in gloom.
The waters of the Nile are agitated as witnessed by the moon.
The boats complain about an eerie silence.
Nobody likes the loneliness on the banks of the Nile.
The eyes of the birds are red.
The Nile is sad.

The stars promise an early end of darkness
But the morning does not show up
The sun is under the cover of chaos and confusion
The anger all over the environment dwarfs the reason.
The road reaches a dead end.
The Nile is sad.

It is easy to win a game and a trophy.
But winning over the anger is not easy.
When anger meets anger, violence erupts
The loss of life ensues; and the devil alone rejoices.
Everybody says the violence is bad.
The Nile is sad.

The Sea, Waves, Clouds of Liberty, and Sailors Vanity

I am the sea and green-headed hills surround me.
They used to view their image in my waters and glee.
Nowadays they blame my waters for their denuded slopes.
The problem is not with my water, which is a bounty of hope.

I envy hills of their monumental heights.
However, my waves stay cool, and dance day and night.
The waves elbow small droplets to work independently and rise.
The violin the air plays, wins the ocean's prestigious prize.

I thrill as the rains fall over my head; and waves too enjoy and play.
The water bubbles smile, while children make crackers to burst, with wet clay.
Wiping out tears of fear is not easy, and it is difficult to catch and send dreadful beasts to the zoo.
There is no point to punish cheetahs for crimes, which leopards frequently, do.

Forget, the notions of rise and obscurity, virtuous is the sense of equanimity.
The feeling of thirst is common; for one reason or the other, everyone is thirsty.
Though I am the sea, I cannot drink my own water, which is salty and undrinkable.
Only can I try to quench my thirst with rains, and my thirst is insatiable.

The air breeze, laden with water droplets, invites the clouds of liberty.
They are messengers of peace, love, friendship and human dignity.
The romanticism of lovely couples outwits the sporadic and spontaneous showers.
They firmly hold their chests together and closet their emotions in the life's theater.

A human-propelled yacht rides on the popular waves of democracy.
The winds of change and wisdom display an exemplary intimacy.
The headwinds are fierce but sailors' vanity prevails.
The yacht reaches the shore; and sailors in a bar, rock and roll.

A sailor from the crew cried, 'I want to leap like a dolphin'
I also want to show my fins.
I don't envy their berth in the heavens,
But I want to build, my own paradisiac mansion.

Water

Water is life and Life is Water

The human race has no present or future without the water.
The fresh water resources are not unlimited.
The potable water supply to villages and cities is inadequate;

The water is life and the life is water.
The life is unthinkable without the water.
The climate has changed:
Which the hopes of people has shattered.
The heat waves sweep all over the world.
The Rivers are dry; and the wildlife die.
The shortage of water forces wild animals to quit their den.
They come inside a city and a village;
Garb an infant, and run away; and face public's wrath and rage.
The struggle for survival continues:
The beast no longer likes the cage.

Inadequate water supply gets people into a brawl.
The powerful call the shots.
The weak and down trodden just stagnate and rot.
At the end of a long queue, after a night long wait.
By the time it is their turn, the supply at the point evaporates.
Inequality in access to short-supply,
Instead of friendly talks, cause neighbors quarrel.
Often the duels turn into riots and that people kill one another
is a sordid tale.

The weak and down trodden become sick and pale
As they recourse to a non-potable water source.
The bonds between the water and life break down.
The diseases germinate.

The adults, youth, children and elders cripple.
The span of life for everybody dwindles.

The climax of story arrives.
People are sad, but the water mafia is happy with the crises.
The water vendors seize opportunities to make quick bucks.
They charge heftily for a bucket which sells due to dire need and people's bad luck,
And blame politicians for the dilapidated infra, pipelines and pumps.

The politicians in power are equally opportunists.
They leave no brick unturned to sway voters to ensure the reelection.
Knowing well there is no money to offer "freebies" in the coffers,
They make water free for everyone.
The rich who can pay, pay to none.
In miles the queues run;
Lucky ones get a few buckets.
The water department runs in perpetual debt.
The staff do not get salaries due to a leader's decision which is inept.

The Tradition of Sharing Water

We are on a mission away from the city.
A hot summer day, it is a pity!
We view crops and harvested grains.
Heaps of chickpeas spread over the terrain.
The electrons flow into homes without an obstruction.
The women are happy to cook and children read at night.
And girls score more than boys in a healthy fight.

We visit an Arab farmer's home.
His dwelling is his pride just as a King's in the Rome.

He serves us eggplants, roasted turkey and dates.
Everyone loves the delicious food.
Nobody hates the food.

The food is plenty but disappears quickly.
The hungry lions devour turkeys to fill their belly.
The refrigerated water is a scarce commodity.
It is a bottle to be shared by all of us equally.

The bottle changes hands from the left to right.
After the drink, everybody expresses thanks and delight.
Unlike a tail-ender on a water pipe, I get my share.
We learn a tradition of sharing water and taking care.

Men and Wildlife

Shadows

The thunderstorm was noisy, the breeze was cool; and nature in green hue dressed up smartly.
The day, hearing the songs that birds sang, retired in the lap of sky peacefully.

The Shadows, wearing black gowns were quickly out, and human faces in the darkness lost dignity.
Some were forced into sex; and some to peddle drugs in the city for younger lots.

The Shadows debunked the myth that human beings even if they wish could never be like God.
The trails in the forest reserves showed a few foot prints of wildlife due to cruelty of poachers.

The Shadows created hubs of greed with maze of rules and

spokes of the money minded manipulators.
The unethical game that predators played became a success due to perfunctory attitudes of the protectors.
The Shadows left the jockeys in the shanty towns themselves to fend-off, and in the down town built concrete structures.
No wonder the shanty spaces became a fertile field to breed and multiply traitors in the network of terror.
The Shadows hired the vulnerable lots to emotions and created an infantry of terror.

They demolished threads of human existence: symbols, values, dignity, and demeanor.
The Shadows created the institutions of inequality and structures to perpetrate injustice to maintain their status and supremacy.

As there was injustice and still there is a lot of inequality increasing faster in terms of income and opportunities.
The stars challenged the Shadows and sparks of hope dispersed in all directions and excluding none.
Seeing the spectacle, Shadows being fear-stricken ran towards the thickets, as chased by angry hounds.

Poaching Under Clouds

The king lion prefers death to eating rats.
It likes a prey which is juicy and fat.
It goes on hunting until that falls flat.

Fearing the king, gazelles move in groups, are alert. If needed, they can quickly run.
They have adapted to run faster than the past generation.
The scorching heat drives them to a lake where they cool off and have a drink.
That is the spot where a lion comes to hunt its prey:

Seeing a lion,
Their lungs lose breath and hearts sink,
But thanks to strategy and tactics, they survive the assault.

Though they never hang out,
Every morning in a compound that looks like an abandoned pagoda,
The lions and gazelles together sing in melodious chorus.
"What a glorious day!"
Gazelles implore the lions to give up the beastly instinct and live, in peace, with other animals.
Do the lions care?

The birds break their night long fast with grains they pick from the hives of ants.
The owl breaks its vow of silence,
And states that
The greens are an illusion in the parched lands;
And for people in poor nations.
As there is no rain, the temperatures soar.
There are no commercial enterprises to work for, earn a little money, and live on.

Zebras think that they are lucky
As they don't have to work in the villages like donkeys.
Grass tastes like charcoal, as their bodies burn,
And eyes to wipe out tear wink.
They thank nature for a suit of black and white stripes,
But ask, why don't they have horns?

It looks like the lake is decorated by pink roses,
But these are flamingos whose beautiful legs are pink like the roses.
They take-off flight in the formation, piercing white clouds in the blue sky.
The streams of hot springs rush into the lake;

And warm waters inspire the Flamingos to copulate and multiply.
The sight is just spectacular, natural, and pleasing to human eyes.

Unable to take a leap, hippopotamus, in a crowded pool, are afloat like huge boulders.
They rise up to breathe in air; a bird enjoys a ride on their shoulders.
As they sink in water again, the bird is nervous and flies away from the beast, out of fear.
Though they are killed by poachers for tusk and meat, the hippo compares well with an ethnic warrior.

To guard their horn and honor, Rhinos hide in the bush from a poacher's trap and an evil eye.
But the poachers find them somehow, and kill;
And ship the horns to a Far East nation
Whose people use in the preparation of the erotic medicines.

Baboons hate eating the cupcakes dropped by reckless tourists,
And jackals have nothing to share, of which they are proud of.
Ostriches no longer hide their heads in the sand, as popularly said.
The hyenas keep its hunting plans secret covered in a shroud.

The elephants suffer, as they cannot fill their trunk with little water left out in the pond, to quench their thirst.
Their life is cut short by shadows,
And poachers who design traps to kill elephants and steal their tusk.
Poachers throw poisonous pumpkins which, elephants eat and meet an untimely death.
The money from the sale of ivories finances a regional war, gluttonous greed, and lust for sex.

The poaching thrives as among the poachers, politicians, and bureaucrats there exists a nexus;
The poaching continues because the punishment to a poacher is not harsh, exemplary and strict.
The poaching continues because the rule of law is compromised by the unethical temptations, and selfish motives.
The poaching continues because the ivory's use in jewelry and medicines the governments permit.

Liberty and Leadership

Hopes of the present century are: responsible and ethical leaders, opportunities, clean air, no tear, no fear, and no intolerances.

Breeze of Liberty

Liberty is an idea to celebrate worldwide.
It is an idea for everybody to feel the great and proud.
It is the value to celebrate and espouse.
It is the 'God particle' for a democratic cause.

Liberty is a license for human dignity and enterprise.
It is the free mindset from the prejudice, pessimism, and bias.
It inspires us to claw a way out of the iron cage.
It is a beacon of light for souls who suffer in the modern age.

It is an antidote to tyranny, torture and trepidation.
It is the 'Arab Spring', victory and finally celebration!
It reinforces probity and roots out corruption.

It is the "Curiosity", adventure, and the Martian connection.

Liberty is a mantra to reconcile the extreme positions.
It gives us chance to reflect, rephrase and hit the equilibrium.
It is the technology to debate issues before taking a decision.
It is the way to nirvana from conflicts and deadly collisions.

Liberty is the yoga to extract non-truth from an obvious truth.
It is an instrument to scoop truth from a web of the untruth.
It is a lesson to learn on the battlefield before firing a missile.
It is the God's nectar to sip, to celebrate, and to smile.

Liberty is a breeze to cool off the radical and negative mindsets.
It lets them breathe fresh air at dawn, at midnight and at the sunset.
It is the force to put them into orbit of sublime imagination.
It supports the dissent against the throttled voice and expression.

Liberty is a diamond necklace that women wear and adore.
They enjoy equal opportunity without an injury and sore.
It is a diamond ring to flaunt the beau of her dreams.
It is the freedom to study and profess any philosophical stream.

Liberty is the enlightenment that Buddha received on the full moon day.
He was not ordinary but a young prince of the day.
He liberated us from the pains of suffering and sorrow;
And he gave us a remedy to live peacefully today and tomorrow.

Liberty is a smile of our neurons.
Its glow shines our face.
Its rays radiates from the face.
Liberty is above a religion, color and race.
It's priceless piece of art on the earth;
It is an adorable deity to worship in eternity in every birth.

Leaders Do Dumb Things!

When they believe
The count of followers on the social media, have their ego a boost.
However, the followers could be bought and sold on the social media through the bots.
Leaders do dumb things!

When the leaders don't try to know their constituents,
The projects and programs are thrown in the air
Contrary to what the followers want.
Addressing issues in the cosmic domain.
Leaders should remain on the earthly terrain.
People need liquid assets to meet immediate needs
Rather than the promises of goodies in the next life.
As leaders don't follow the public mood,
People drift en masse away from such leaders;
And at the ballot box, they switch loyalties to give chance to the other leaders.
Leaders do dumb things!

When the leaders switch loyalty and their party before or after a general election

Lured by an offer of a cabinet rank or a lucrative portfolio.
The followers learn the dynamic to switch loyalty from such leaders.
Leaders present no ideal or standard of probity to followers.
They would easily retract from a stated position or what they earlier said about a rival and an issue.
The public loses trust in such individuals and the leadership.
Leaders do dumb things!

When they abdicate a hard-won responsibility in sheer stupidity,
They act by their ambitions rather than the public opinion and rationality.
The public does not trust such leaders for they squander the opportunity.
Leaders do dumb things!

When they falsely accuse and implicate a rival for corrupt practices that destroys their esteem.
Losing a bid devastates the dreams.
They are challenged by an aggrieved party in the court,
Gripped by fear of prosecution,
They tender unconditional apologies.
But the retraction from what they said publicly,
Smashes their reputation.
They present themselves unworthy for public trust.
The collaborators resign in protest.
You name it, on every platform in print or on social media,
They are ridiculed and trolled;
They become laughing stocks.
Leaders do dumb things!

When they don't like the collaborators criticizing and challenging their position and opinion.
They tolerate such individuals as long as possible, but eventually fire them.
The chemistry does not work, moreover, the truth of matter is:

The leaders of narcissistic nature want the "Yes Men,"
Leaders do dumb things!

When they favor their relatives and award a lucrative supply contract; jobs; and key positions in the government.
The public hate them; and is angry and frustrated for their love for nepotism.
The leaders of this breed amass wealth, keeping all the power in their hands.
Such leaders build unethical alliances;
And their rise to power is marked by deceit and back stabbing.
The development agenda is dumped, which they announced at the hustings.
Leaders do dumb things!

When they strategically avoid speaking against colleagues who are tainted in scams.
By being silent, they let such people store money in the coffers
However, not speaking against a crime is the same as abetting the crime.
And the covering up of a guilty act is also a crime.
The public which was promised "zero tolerance" for corruption feels betrayed.
Leaders do dumb things!

When they keep the "keeps," and indulge in the promiscuous relationships behind the closed doors.
Even before the electoral results are out, the mistress leaves the country, anticipating the defeat.
However, a chaste wife stays with him
Though instead of love, she often suffers humiliation, injuries, and insults.
 Leaders do dumb things!

When they wage war on the basis of wrong assumptions.

However, war is never a route for peace, as proven by a continuous turmoil in the Middle East.
When minds think of war; the war happens.
Peace will prevail, if minds desire peace and stay calm.
Truly, it is wisely said by a proverb, "we can see as far as our thoughts see,"
Leaders do dumb things!

When leaders gossip, speak lies, and indulge in mongering rumors,
Though such acts are forbidden by every faith, yet leaders like these things
As tools to confuse the public and sway the public opinion.
They take public for granted, but the public is not a child.
Leaders do dumb things!

When their misdeeds and greed betray the public trust
For the compromise on national security, and commit high crimes of misdemeanor.
Their actions make them the objects of public concern, criticism and satire.
 Even so, their followers adore them and admire.
They forget that the public punish a leader who is a liar.
Leaders do dumb things!

Leaders use religion to garner public support and sympathy.
People get frustrated when the religion fails to solve their economic issues.
Leaders use rhetoric, make bold promises, and leave them there to guess, dream and hope.
Leaders walk on the slippery slopes.
Leaders do dumb things!

Voters Do Dumb Things too!

When they elect leaders based on identities,
It shows they regard identities more than an inclusive agenda of progress, peace, and prosperity,
As they vote for identity,
The leadership becomes institutionalized in a political family
Not only has a baton passed from father to son or father to daughter,
Every family member is elected to be a leader.
Politics is a trademark profession.
Voters do dumb things too!

When they elect criminals as leaders;
Leaders as criminals survive and criminals as leaders thrive.
They hatch conspiracies and clears the way from adversaries.
The politics becomes an out of bound territory for gentlemen.
While the poor sit on the fringes, political elites prevail.
Voters do dumb things too!

When they opt for business as usual,
Identity based biases, bullies, violence, corruption, favoritism, and nepotism will prevail.
Nothing changes; People get frustrated.
But every political party is happy with the status quo because the system as it is, serves everybody's interests.
Identities that are left out agitate for a share of the pie and clash with the system.
Leadership succumbs to pressures and grants them concessions.
Voters do dumb things too!

When they elect leaders
Whom interests are in conflict with public interests.
Leaders may tweak public policies to suit their commercial needs.
While they benefit,

Public eventually loses by having dumb leaders.
Voters do dumb things too!

They Fear Will Lose the Election

Politicians calumniate their rivals: They identify enemies, demonize, and insinuate them of scandals, and corruptions to add value to their fame. If they don't do this, they fear will lose the election.

Young politicians want to displace the old guards. They want to change the old notions. Irresponsibly accusing opponents, they challenge them in the public space. If they don't do this, they fear will lose the election.

But they never apply the same rules to them; always evade accountability and scrutiny. When questioned, they blame the vendetta politics to trick the public. If they don't do this, they fear they will lose the election.

Having sensed the public opinion is not in their favor,
As part of strategy, they have a rival's server compromised. They use the critical information to benefit them. If they don't do this, they fear will lose the election.

Should We Trust Such a Leader?

My impressions about leadership emanate from observations and interactions with individuals, families and friends in several countries and all of these go into answering this question: How to Judge a Leader?

When the actions deviate from the spoken words,
You might call it what you might prefer to,
There is something strange about it
It is hypocrisy.
Should we trust such a leader?

When he twists his lips,
While speaking, his tongue often trips.
You can say that he is telling a lie!
But he does everything to conceal it and deny.
Should we trust such a leader?

When he slings mud at his opponents;
He fails to substantiate charges he made against them;
He is sued in the court.
Being fearful of the conviction, not only he retracts what he said;
He tenders unconditional apologies for his deliberate acts.
Should we trust such a leader?

When he often changes the pitch of his voice
In the meetings, while others seriously deliberate, he rejoices.
He is saying something that he does not mean.
His demeanor is strange.
Should we trust such a leader?

She is steadfast to "principles" and has an unaverred mind.
She decides to favor public and to harm none
She rises to demand and fight for justice
She is above the greed and emotional caprice.
She holds tight in her hands a weighing scale and a sword.
She is maker of her image and destiny; and she is a deity, a temple's lord.
Should we trust such a leader?

When his compassionate heart blooms like a cherry blossom.
He lifts many up from a pyramid's bottom.

Some of his hypotheses fail the tests of the empiricism
For which he attracts positive criticism,
But his open mindedness and charismatic nature earn him fame.
Should we trust such a leader?

Before you trust, know your leader's virtues and wiles.
Never get swayed away by their similes and smiles.

A Giant of History

Mandela was a statesman; and a giant of history.
He changed the depressed minds to brim with hope and liberty.
He was a beacon in the darkness of the refulgent light.
He led the South African struggle against the apartheid.
He was a star of hope to millions.
His funeral attracted condolences of billions.

His body was caged for twenty seven years in the Robben Island.
But his spirit could not be imprisoned by the oppressors' iron hands.
It remained free and indomitable.
The spirit needs no correction, because it is complete;
It is conscientious and able.

He abandoned hatred against his people's tormentors.
He defeated the apartheid, and forgave its perpetrators,
In other words, he showered love and compassion to his oppressors,
Though it wasn't expected of him.
Ordinarily people, however, do tit for tat.
He hated the sins of the white men against the South African people, but not the sinners.

This is what the founder of Jainism suggested.
He invigorated life in the values essential for human co-existence.
And he wrote a new doctrine, based on "Truth and Reconciliation"
It bodes well of an African proverb, "go together if you want to go far."

His steadfastness and patience were keys to his success and glory.
He remained committed to and tirelessly worked for his dream, this tells his story.
He endured innumerable tremors of insult, injury, suffering and pain.
His sacrifices are not to go in vain.

The challenge is:
Can we learn from Mr. Mandela's legacy? Can we have more of leaders of Mandela's caliber in Africa?

Between Giants and Dwarf

I am a star between the giants and dwarfs.
I repair whatever is broken in human hearts.
I am the source of life and intelligence.
I destroy a drunken devil of darkness.

I give strength to the weak and down-trodden.
I inspire them to look beyond a tiny horizon.
I teach them how, in the troubled time, they should cope.
I tell them to ring the bell for peace, friendship and hope.

I exhort waves to not fear, but rise high to a clarion call.

Life is short; it is "to live and to let others live," after all.
I tell corals in the sea, to hum like a jungle bee.
I tell the young to run, just for passion and glee.

I tell the storm to shake hands with the mountains and be calm.
The grass crushed by elephants fighting for a territory, groans and needs to be supplied balm.
I tell the moon to reach out the victims of violence, hatred and grudge.
The breeze of liberty revives hope in the disappointed souls through message of peace and love.

I reverse my polarity to refresh my energy, look and image.
I advise people to not rush in anger and contemptuous rage.
I live up to and uphold the moral bounds of the nature.
I bend the space-time continuum, and create a curvature.
I am a star between giants and dwarfs.

Shooting in a Texas Church

To attend the church service, people assemble in a pious mood;
And they sing and dance to devotional tunes, while in the portico, there are some dogs barking.
In the shadows, a devil casts a net of terror and guns down over thirty persons.
Bullets turn the place into ruins with bloody marks.
Shootings do happen every now and then, but people let them pass.

The abode of peace and freedom, devils are allowed to trespass.
It seems the leaders prefer to leave alone the root cause of the disease, but try to treat the symptoms.
Flames of hope are doused by the hateful venom.

Motivation

Desires and Dreams

Billions of youth aspire to achieve certain things in their life.
They desire to get a fulfilling job, a healthy environment and a debonair husband or a beautiful wife.

The desires are like seeds of joy buried underneath the soil
Which continue to remain dormant under the rock,
Unless it gracefully rains and moistens their dry cloak.

Desires appear like bamboo shoots after the rain.
Too many desires lead one to astray.
Desires die as footprints disappear on the golden coast.
Emotionally charged minds swing between despair and hope.
A new desire is born in the next moment.

The unfulfilled ones on the memory lane leave dents.
The dents are a few regrets; and the human spirit is a little bit damp.
The mist fills the space in the morning air; and there is a little bit of chill.
The moisture dries out as the rising sun glitters the hill.

Breeze ripples a new expectation in order for the vacuum to fill.

Choose your dream, your desire, and thus, bless the life with happiness;
Choose the stillness of a deep lake to pacify a crowd of ionized emotions;
Choose a broad minded imagination and realism of revelations;
Choose the wisdom beyond the book; beyond the eyes through self-introspection.

Willpower

The luck knocks at the door on a glorious day.
A hidden force tilts balance in favor of a passionate doer at end of the day.
The efforts and willpower bring a desire to fruition.
Which otherwise is waste flushed in the drain.

Without willpower, desires are just the chaotic conditions of a whirlpool.
Without willpower, desires are invisible rays, and do not glorify the soul.
Willpower provides a concrete platform for ideas to shape into an edifice.
Willpower acts as a mason of eminence.

Without willpower, desires creep, cripple and crawl.
Without willpower, desires lose context and ground.
Without willpower, the inertia drags a life's journey.

Without willpower, one is fearful; and one naturally blames destiny.

Willpower strengthens the heart through its powerful rays.
Willpower is the most powerful weapon in a person's armory.
Willpower is a sharp knife's edge to cut such temptations that are unhealthy.
Willpower inspires us to know what is desirous and worthy.

Knowledge

Knowledge enlightens the road to fulfillment of goals.
So, better have it even at the expense of family gold.
Knowledge expands by donating it to others.
Unshared knowledge collects dust just as the books well arranged on the shelf but remain untouched.

Knowledge is what the Greek proverb says: "Having received the torch, you can pass it on?"
Knowledge gives us wisdom to know the difference between action and inaction.

Action versus Inaction

To desire and dream is good, but it is said that
 "Without pain, there is no gain"
A conscientious man makes an effort to perform an action.
Action without willpower is halfhearted effort and thus inaction.

Taking action is a virtue and inaction a vice.

Do not give up your virtue under any circumstance.
Taking action is living a life and inaction death.
While living, earn people's goodwill and avoid their wrath.

Taking action is courage and inaction cowardice.
Divine help comes to a courageous man to accomplish all that he decides.
Taking action is to implement an idea and inaction a problem of attitude.
So, give up your defiance to change and procrastination to win over the attitude.

Taking action is a celestial vow and inaction a straw.
Keep expanding your boundaries and do not stop at a game's draw.
Taking action is wisdom and inaction invites depression.
One's legacy is all about leaving behind one's footprints and impressions.

Taking action is" karma" and inaction forbidden.
One needs to extract inaction from action and action an inaction.
Taking a pure action is valor and wisdom and inaction sheer foolishness.
A man of wisdom and valor wins every game of life by his steadfastness.

Empathy

The world will be a better place to live for everybody

Everybody celebrates culture and cherishes festivities, parties, food, and good moments. It is normal, but if your culture celebrates my culture and mine celebrates yours, the world will be a better place to live for everybody.

People are sick, fearful, and distraught by the pervading smog in the sky. The people want to expel the smog from cities and life. If someone can transmute the smoggy molecules to bubbles of oxygen, the world will be a better place to live for everybody.

The men play sports to tame animals like bulls to prove their worth, vanity, and velour. But if they can control their animal instincts, there will be no cases of human trafficking, rapes and sexual harassment. The world will be a better place to live for everybody.

The young people may be tempted to trick a gentleman, cheat on a girl or friends, pick a pouch of drugs or jump to hard drinks. Is this behavior praiseworthy? But amidst the temptations, if they do not compromise their integrity and character, and remain unmoved like a mountain, the world will be a better place to live for everybody.

There is light at the end of tunnel, so "keep your fingers crossed." While being in the tunnel, if you can avoid having a

"Tunnel Vision," the world will be better place to live for everybody.

The things that are deemed to happen will happen, but do not let anyone ever control your thoughts. If you can change the world with your thoughts for good of the aged, disabled, poor and voiceless people, the world will be a better place to live for everybody.

I see an infant poking a little finger in the electric socket. She is an innocent one. Like a child, if you can stop fearing the unknown, and create a new world to include everyone in it, the world will be a better place to live for everybody.

Let new ideas be born like bubbles in the rains. If you can measure their worth for community before they are burst, the world will be a better place to live for everybody.

Discriminatory Empathy

The human mind empathizes the loved ones who receive an injury in an accident or suffer from a protracted illness.
We empathize because they concern us.
But our brains do not feel complete pain and emotions that an individual experiences.
Human beings are much less empathetic to those who are unrelated to them.
People watch, as mere spectators, the ordeal of a young girl being physically abused by criminals in the public square in day light because she does not belong to them.
The crimes against women happen because the criminals think they can buy everything with their money so they don't fear the law.
The crime continues because the conviction is not quick, and punishment is not exemplary.

The police condones the incident and do not register her complaint, and compromise the law, if the victim is a voiceless person of the society.
The human brains don't grieve for victims of the terror attacks if these incidents do not concern them and happen in their part of world.
I don't care attitude dismisses an empathetic thought.
The discriminatory empathy polarizes the society in the communities of dislikes and likes.
When the underdogs are repressed above limit, violent protests against the leaders spike.
Can we switch from a discriminatory empathy to non-discriminatory empathy to show our compassion and love to those who are unrelated to us?

Case of Marathwada Farmers

The cotton plants looked like brown bamboos erected to scare crows away.
Like skin of farmers, the underneath grass turned pale, but don't ask me how?
Everybody talks of drought as nature's fury equally hurting the high and low.
The rich farmers have muscles to bear losses, but the poor have no resilience to run the show.

The poor borrow money from lenders at rates found in fiction and history books.
One wonders, who regulates such rates and how in modern times, thrive such crooks.
The poor unable to repay debts, execute a self-announced judgement to take their life.
 Their souls have liberation from a life insulted by a money lender and injured by nature.

Drought is not a onetime event; it visits the Marathwada region every now and then.
A story appears on the plight of farmers in daily newspapers, caused by lack of rains.
The readers cry foul; sympathize and paint a picture of gloom in their memory lane.
But the next morning, the story becomes old and newspaper is trashed in the dustbin.

What astonishes me is the apathy to the farmers' suffering from crucifying pain.
But, the least they deserve is our prayers for a few short rains.
There is a solution and technology to fix this problem, but the issue is: who can?
The one who empathizes with the farmers will take appropriately certain actions.

Case of Street Dogs

Tired of a night long vigil,
Dogs are quiet, and a tad civil.
They guard in the night the street;
Though them none ever greets.
They keep the thieves at bay.
But in the neighborhood committees
They don't have any say.
They do a volunteer's work to make the area safe.
They really starve,
They don't have bins of grains.
Nor do they have money to buy the cakes.

They nap in the little burrows,
On a mattress of misty soil
That keeps them happy and cool.
Some of them sleep on the benches

Like homeless people do in the metropolises.
However, the lucky hounds find a home in the ranches.

Fatigue intoxicates their spinal cord,
Like a fresh wine of the sort.
Dogs soon pass out.
Though bugs bite their skin deep and hard,
Dogs just fling the tail to keep the bugs away and far.

But if they hear a little bang;
They promptly break the sleep and challenge the intruder's audacity.
They sleep less, but work more, that is a trait of their personality.
This is a habit worthy of emulation by a student in her personality.

After they wake up
They straighten their limbs.
They walk and play together, and have fun.
They play like kids do,
Few drills that they do make the fat burn.

The crazy lots roam on the street;
And guard their territory from an intruders reach.
When an alien dog enters the territory, they get perturbed.
Until that one is driven out
They bark at a stretch;
And refuse to shut down.

When they see a dog in a collar and chained.
As water boils in the kettle, the blood boils in their brain.
And they bark, as if they demand the owner to unleash their kin.
But the master rebukes them for a loud and an insisting tone.

Still crazier, they race barking behind a running car

Until the car is out of sight.
Eventually they realize the futility, and stop.
They put their heads down after a flop show,
But there is merit in setting up a higher goal.

The men and women suffering from the malefic effects of the planets worship a black dog.
Suggested by a "Guru," they offer the dog some tasty rolls,
Sensing an underlying trick in the food being served, dogs do not eat.
And the rolls litter the pathways.

The street dogs roam here and there;
The environment makes them sturdy and wiser.
A man will bash if you call him a dog.
However, some traits of a dog, are divine.
The dog is faithful to its owner, and is full of patience.
It silently gazes; and waits until the owner serves him meal.
The dog provides a round the clock vigilance of master's family and home.
After the master has passed away, the dog guards his or her tomb.
Could you adopt a puppy?

Doesn't Nature Deserve an Empathy?

What is this noise?
Little Rayva asks me,
I tell her this:
This is the noise coming from air conditioners, ambulances, firefighters, airplanes, cars and Lorries.

She says the noise is horrible.

I tell her, children cry
As parents ask them to rise up and get ready for the school.
Like this noise bothers you, children's cries disturb the parents.

She asks further:

Do trees cry? Do rivers cry?; Do wildlife cry?; and Does the earth cry?
I say, yes

Nature, wildlife and earth cry bitterly when human beings rip them off to satiate greed.
Why cannot we hear her cries?
Nature wails but we don't hear because there are noises in our consciousness; and in the background of our existence.
Nature feels like a lost child at an abandoned harbor
Where there is no one to talk to, and there is nobody to take care of her; and there is no benefactor.
Nature is hot and angry;
If we fail to pacify her she will burn all of us.

How can we pacify nature?
We have to show some concern to nature's predicament and stand by her side like we do to our family in the time of trouble;
And address threats to coexistence.

Darkness

When a suspicion camouflages with trust, mind disbelieves
Even though a few phrases appear progressive, agenda is touted to comprise of inconsistent promises

By those who fear their traditions and culture will see an incursion by inimical elements
Because every now and then zealots abuse them, as reports a daily newspaper.
The intolerant rhetoric and violent moods show such persons are in a stupor caused by preconceived notions.
Which dilute everybody's desire of living together.

The narrative is hopeful,
But the message is received with skepticism in a heterogeneous society.
And it is unsurprising.
The vulnerable communities need reassurances from the leadership.
Shouldn't we hold hands so that they should willingly discard fear, alienation and anxiety?

Like the air needs to be cleared of toxic gases and particulate matters,
Minds need to be liberated from stereotypes of religious dogmas, race, cultures, caste, and creeds;
And all of us need to meditate and pray for enlightenment of empathy in order to
Remove darkness from society in the way peasant's worthless weeds.

Else Change your Template

Some people believe that they are great; it is fine if you think that way, as long as you do not treat others as if they are inferior to you. Else change your template.

The faithful people believe that their faith is pure, and eternal. There is no problem, as long as they do not kill the believers of other faiths. Else change your template.

That they will live forever is the biggest illusion of human beings though it is observed that there is someone disappearing from the scene every now and then in this world. The breath stops quite unpredictably like a bubble bursts in the water. If you believe in the impermanence of human existence, else change your template.

Some people get angry at a slight provocation, they humiliate parents if they question them or deny their demands. You should accept that "no tree gives shelter to angry birds.", else change your template.

An injured man is dying on the road; nobody dares to stare, let alone care of him. What would you call it? An example of extreme selfishness and disrespect for human life and dignity. As they extend no helping hand, people deny them a chance to perform a noble deed. If you reject to being a silent spectator next time, else change their template.

By showing apathy to a dying destitute, people show an indifferent attitude, but rationalize the inaction. But they were indeed unkind. We don't realize the attitude problem, unless we are told. If you accept to fix your attitude, else change the template.

To not help others when they are in dire need, but would like to be helped in their hour of need is how the selfish men behave. The extreme selfishness leads to greed. Extreme greed causes grave injustice to neighbors and society. If you appreciate the above adage, else change your template.

Wealth creates illusions: the rich think that they can buy everything with their wealth. But the rich cannot buy life's time and happiness, nor can they buy peace of mind. They cannot rent a surrogate to suffer on their behalf when they are in pain. If you agree to the above, else change your template.

Living without Grace

Living without grace is a total time pass.
A person who lives like that is an ass.
He does work well for others.
But he does not light up a lamp in his own yard.
Life is stuffed with mundane things.
The sound of temple bell bypasses his ear even if it loudly rings.

Living without grace is living like stones at the river bed.
The stones don't realize that the river is flowing over their head.
The stones suspect the river's intent to lift them up.
They blame the dancing fish for their problems, and the stunning bubbles.

They like to mock efforts to spread love and peace.
They don't learn on their own, nor do they form the experience of others.
They see malice in everything: the shells, waves, boats, and sailors.
Everybody beseeches them to change your attitude to life.

Living without grace is like a family to board an aero plane,
But leaves its luggage behind.
Frustrated, instead of reflecting on its folly,
It misdirects its anger at the airline staff and coolie.

Living without grace is like a life being discounted faster than the lifeless assets.
The person living without grace identifies new ways of hate, anger and frown.

Living without grace is like traversing the boundaries of demeanor.
However, Nature lives within her boundaries. The oxygen molecules though they freely float in, but don't escape the atmosphere.

Living without grace is like making holes in the vessel you are sailing.
Living without grace is like ripping off nature to satisfy personal greed far beyond the needs.
Living without grace is like leading an unsustainable life on this planet,
Which is like a man is cutting a tree branch upon which he is sitting.
Living without grace is like dumping your rubbish in front of your neighbor.
Living without grace is disrespecting your guests and visitors.
Living without grace is like trampling on the honor of a woman.
Living without grace is like betraying the country of your birth.
Living without grace is like risking your dignity to greed.

Beyond the Eyes

Time

Time is intangible; time is singular.
Time is eternal; it is not comprehended by a common mind.

One who understands time, is a person of different kind.
Just like a river, it perennially flows; it never reverses.
Time never stops.
However, it is definite. Whoever is born today is bound to stop one day.
Everybody enjoys the happy hours, but everybody has to pass testing times.
Time checks the reality of everyone:
Those who fail the test, face the fury of time.
One who passes the test, time confers upon him or her, according to merit, a rank.
Time cannot be stored in barrels or in the coffers of a bank.

Note!

Breath

The air that we breathe in and breathe out is imperceptible to the eyes too.
No one is required to pay to inhale it or stand in a queue.
It is the divine grace that God has made it equitably available to everyone.
It sustains our life on this planet; and it is source of the "Origin of Species."
It flows like the mercy of God in our body. It is not an illusion.
But human beings take the air for granted and do not take care of it.
They pollute the air with toxic gases and particulate matters.
A life span reduces due to the polluted air;
The human life ceases to exist in the absence of air.

Sanctify!

Eternal Rest

Death is a universal truth,
Everybody accepts it but does not take it seriously.
It is inescapable;
Its time is uniquely fixed for everyone residing on this planet,
When the time comes; as God withdraws his mercy, human beings slip in to eternal rest.
But the deaths caused by terrorists are unacceptable, untimely and unnatural.

God of death is impartial to everyone.
A person's rank does not matter before Him.
Skin color does not impress Him.
Name and wealth acquired at the birth do not sway His decision.
Everybody who starts with big or humble beginning comes to an end.
The pain of leaving everything behind hurts.

God forbids hiring a person to die in place of the other person.
The substitution is prohibited: An old man cannot die for a young child or newly born.
Death equalizes the earthly differences between the rich and poor.

God of death mocks powerful persons when they exploit the trodden and poor.
God of death mocks leaders for they fail to remove differences between the rich and poor.
He corrects that in His own way.

Realize!

Eternal Matter

There is a thing that pervades in the universe,
It encircles; and it envelopes the whole existence.
It encompasses everything that makes the universe.
What is it?
It is invisible to human eyes;
And opaque even to the human-designed sensors.
It cannot be annihilated. It is eternal.
What is it?

Inquire!

Eternal Beats

Time hides the sounds produced at the creation of the universe.
These are the eternal beats that are inaudible to human ears.
The persons of rare genes who wander like homeless men in the universe,
Try to hear the eternal beats in meditation; they narrate the experience.
The identities disappear;
The possessions that were sources of vanity, lose luster.
And furthermore,
Hearing the eternal beats is a prelude to understanding the eternal matter.

Hear!

Eternal Fragrance

The earthly fragrances make us feel good.
The cosmic fragrance is ethereal and eternal.
It not only nourishes our heart, body, and mind,
It blesses us all and makes our life happy and fulfilled.
It is universal. Like air, it touches every soul and our whole existence.
It flows inside me; inside everybody and everywhere.

It permeates through pores in the body and soul of a true seeker.
The eternal fragrance is intangible, however, its effects appear tangible:
It guides persons who sense its aroma to travel the road to eternal fame.

Inhale!

CPSIA information can be obtained
at www.ICGtesting.com
Printed in the USA
BVHW040952170219
540457BV00018B/443/P